Native American Courtship and Marriage

Leslie Gourse

Native Voices
Summertown, Tennessee

Native Voices

Book Publishing Company
P. O. Box 99
Summertown, TN 38483

Printed in the United States

08 07 06 05   4 3 2 1

ISBN-13   978-1-57067-170-8
ISBN-10   1-57067-170-2

"The Legend of the Flute" and "The Serpent of the Sea" from *American Indian Myths and Legends* by Richard Erdoes and Alfonso Ortiz. Copyright © 1984 by Richard Erdoes and Alfonso Ortiz.
Reprinted by permission of Pantheon Books, a division of Random House, Inc.

Gourse, Leslie.
   Native American courtship and marriage / Leslie Gourse.
       p. cm.
   Rev. ed. of: Native American courtship and marriage traditions. c2000.
   Includes bibliographical references and index.
   ISBN 1-57067-170-2
   1. Indians of North America—Marriage customs and rites. 2. Indians of North America—Rites and ceremonies. 3. Indians of North America—Clothing. 4. Courtship—United States—History. I. Gourse, Leslie. Native American courtship and marriage traditions. II. Title.

   E78.M27G68 2004
   306.81'089'97073—dc22

                            2004019648

Printed on recycled paper

The Book Publishing Co. is committed to preserving ancient forests and natural resources. We have elected to print this title on Torchglow Opaque, which is 30% postconsumer recycled and processed chlorine free. As a result of our paper choice, we have saved the following natural resources:

4.2 trees
196 lbs of solid waste
1774 gallons of water
385 lbs of net greenhouse gases
713 kw hours of electricity

We are a member of Green Press Initiative. For more information about Green Press Initiative visit: www.greenpressinitiative.org

CONTENTS

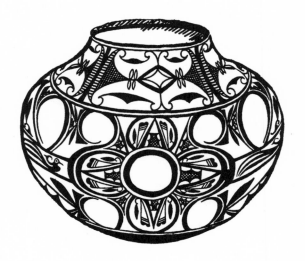

INTRODUCTION

An Unusual Marriage

*P*ocahontas, the favorite daughter of a great Powhatan chief in the territory that would become known as Virginia, contracted a unique marriage for her era on April 5, 1614. In a Christian ceremony, she and Englishman John Rolfe, a tobacco farmer, were married by the senior minister of a Jamestown church. Pocahontas was nineteen years old—already old for a Powhatan maiden to marry. She wore an English wedding dress of fine muslin and a long veil and robe, and around her neck, a string of freshwater pearls—a wedding gift from her father, Chief Powhatan (as the English called him).

Her uncle, a chief of his own village, and two of her brothers attended the wedding. Powhatan, leader of all the Powhatan villages, refused to go himself. The English believed he didn't want to give anyone the impression that he was surrendering his rights to his land in any way. He and the English had fought many battles, and now he simply wanted to live without wars. He knew he couldn't drive the English away from his territories, and he accepted his daughter's choice of a husband. But he was keeping his distance

Pocahontas in an old painting from the National Anthropological Archives, Smithsonian Institution. (Opps Neg 00875C)

from the English and maintaining his dignity as a chief by staying away from the wedding ceremony.

To show his enduring love for his daughter, Powhatan gave the newlyweds some land north of Jamestown on the James River. The couple built a house there and named it "Varina," in honor of the Spanish word for the type of tobacco Rolfe grew.

The governor of Jamestown visited Powhatan one day. The old chief asked him how Pocahontas and Rolfe "lived, loved, and liked."

The governor told Powhatan that the couple was very happy. He seemed pleased and peaceful in his old age. Though the English and the Powhatans still engaged in little skirmishes occasionally, they traded with each other and coexisted. People referred to the time as "the Peace of Pocahontas." So the unusual alliance between the daughter of a chief and a British farmer had great political ramifications.

Probably nobody but Pocahontas, always a very bright and curious child, could have become involved in such a marriage at that time. She had enjoyed a special relationship with the English from the day the first boat landed on Powhatan land. A preadolescent girl accustomed to running around without any clothes (Powhatan girls didn't dress in doeskin skirts until they reached puberty), she became friendly with Captain John Smith, a prominent member of the English expedition. Many times their friendship helped save the lives of the English settlers suffering gruesome hardships, particularly famine and disease, in a strange land. Pocahontas persuaded her father to give corn and small game to the English countless times.

Eventually John Smith had a serious accident. Pocahontas, by then a young lady in a doeskin skirt, with decorative feathers in her hair, mistakenly believed he was dead. He returned to England without saying good-bye to her. She refused to marry an Indian man whom her father wanted her to choose, and she went to live with a relative in a distant village. An Englishman visiting there was surprised to see her. The English didn't know where she had gone. He invited her to have dinner on his boat; when she arrived, he locked her in a room and sailed with her to Jamestown. The Englishman had the bright idea to use her as a pawn in a power struggle and bribe her father to do favors for the English in return for his beloved daughter's release. But Powhatan resisted. He guessed correctly that the English were very grateful to Pocahontas for the kindnesses and favors she had done for them; they would treat her well.

Unable to budge her father, the English soon released Pocahontas from her jail cell. A minister of the church of England, Reverend Alexander Whitaker, who respected Indians, took her to live in his house. He converted Pocahontas to Christianity, although some say she made the decision of her own free will.

Instructed to behave like an English lady, Pocahontas put away her doeskin skirt, beads, and feathers in a closet. Instead she wore a stiff corset made with whalebones, and on top of that she put on a blouse that covered her upper body all the way to her neck. She also wore an ankle-length skirt to conform to English fashion.

Pocahontas was taught to bow her head and look at the ground when she walked in the streets the way Englishwomen did. Fluent in English, she learned to read Christian prayers. The English sent word to King James I in England that an Indian princess had chosen to convert to Christianity. Religious conversions had been one of the major missions of the English. She became known by her baptismal name, Rebecca.

However, Pocahontas wasn't simply a pawn or a prized possession. The English truly liked her for her delightful personality. One Sunday in church, a widower named John Rolfe noticed her and began talking with her, calling her Pocahontas out of respect for her background. Furthermore, he found himself very attracted to the small, dark woman with delicate hands.

Every free moment he had, John Rolfe visited her at Reverend Whitaker's farm. He sat with her in church on Sundays, took walks with her in the tobacco fields, and talked about the beauty of the land. Pocahontas liked Rolfe, too, for his sweet, respectful personality and his curiosity about people and places. Rolfe wanted to marry her and asked the governor of Jamestown whether marriage with a woman who had been born a "heathen" would be acceptable.

The governor was very pleased. He thought the English and Indigenous people distrusted each other because of their struggle for control of the land, and a marriage between a colonist and the daughter of a chief could ameliorate tensions. The governor also hoped that the marriage would encourage more English people to venture to the New World and, most especially, to send more money.

It remained for Pocahontas, her fiancé Rolfe, and other settlers to go to Powhatan's village and ask for his blessing for the marriage. Instead of meeting the boat, Powhatan sent two of his sons, who delivered the message that Powhatan approved of the marriage. He wanted better relations with the English. "I'm tired of fighting," he said.

The families of the couple exchanged gifts—Powhatan gave a little of his land to the newlyweds in return for a peaceful attitude from the English colonists.

Pocahontas/Rebecca lived in the English style. A year after her marriage, she had a baby son, whom she named Thomas in honor of the English governor. Jamestown's financial backers felt so delighted that they set up a financial award as a way of thanking Pocahontas for all the help she had given the colony to ensure its survival in past years; every year the fund paid Pocahontas and her son. She did maintain some of her Powhatan tribal traditions in her daily life in the farmhouse that she and John Rolfe built on the shore of the James River, the land her father had given them. She sang Indian lullabies to her son, tied him to a crib board in the Indian fashion, and propped him up against a wall. That way she could keep an eye on him while she did her chores.

Eventually Pocahontas traveled to England, where she met the colony's financial backers in the Virginia Company, and they presented her to the king and queen at court. Captain John Smith, whom she had believed was dead, paid her a surprise visit in the inn where she was staying. By that time she was weak from an illness— probably pneumonia. His visit excited and agitated her tremendously. She was actually overwhelmed by emotion, because she had been so attached to him. Though she had been only an adolescent when she met him, she had probably fallen in love with him. She was certainly very angry to learn he was alive and had simply never contacted her. She died of pneumonia and was buried in England. Her son, who was raised in England by his father's relatives, didn't return to Jamestown until he was a grown man. Both the English and the Powhatans trusted him, as they had Pocahontas.

Although marriages between Native people and white settlers of European backgrounds did take place as years went on, they never became everyday events. Usually the couples met with none of the acceptance, and their unions entailed none of the rituals and ceremonies that were standard with marriages between Indians in their close-knit communities. Furthermore, well-defined tribal marriage traditions and rites had little in common with those of the Europeans.

Overview: Native Marriage Traditions

Had Pocahontas married an Indian, her father would have received a request for her hand in marriage from a suitable young man—in this case a brave, smart man whom a chief could be proud to have as his son-in-law. The families would meet to exchange gifts. The gifts from the bride's family, if it had means—and Powhatan certainly did—would usually equal the value and even surpass the sumptuousness of the gifts from the groom's people. Horses were often a major gift item in the marriage agreements. In many tribes, when the families exchanged gifts, the couple became formally married. Then the families relaxed with a feast, its lavishness dependent upon the means of the bride's and groom's immediate families and their relatives. (Relatives sometimes added to the bride-prices and the feast foods.) Events, including those in the early courtship days leading up to marriage and continuing through the remainder of the couple's lives, were usually well prescribed in the varied customs and traditions of the different tribes. Some parents contracted marriages, at least informally, when the future brides were still babies and their prospective husbands were already young boys.

Four centuries of American occupation and dominance have eroded the systems that the Indigenous people so carefully worked out and faithfully practiced. These days, many Native American couples who decide to get married seek out a clergyman or a justice of the peace or they go to city hall, as do many others in the country. Rarely do Native Americans delve into their rich heritage of customs and ceremonies for courtship, marriage, and family structure. "They're gone," says an Indian woman who works at the Smithsonian Institution's National Museum of the American Indian in New York. Only the people of the Long House—the Iroquois—and a few Western tribes keep some of their traditions alive, and the Iroquois do it more or less secretly. (Though Indians around the country stage powwows regularly and invite the public, there are still some private celebrations to which the non-Indian public is not invited.) Otherwise, the Native American marriage traditions are relegated to the memories of older people and the history books.

Native people themselves have delivered oral histories about their lives, including courtship, marriage, and related arrangements and rites. One reason so many sources exist is that there have been so many tribes, and the regions in which they have lived necessitated different survival tactics. Consequently, legend and lore and factual accounts vary greatly from region to region and community to community. There are also some books, articles, and sociological and anthropological treatises written by experts on Indian history that help keep the memories alive. Often outside experts have concentrated on one group or region—the Eastern or Southwestern tribes, for example—and have studied their different courtship and marriage traditions. Similarities among them have also emerged, for all the original people of North America have shared some concerns, traditions, and history.

Here are a few examples of Native American family, courtship, and marriage traditions that many tribes have in common.

In general, marriages were arranged by parents who wanted to merge the worldly goods of two families; sometimes these families were already related. It was common for a mother to orchestrate a marriage between her son and her brother's daughter. That was considered a good arrangement and better than having the son marry the daughter of the mother's sister. But incest—a marriage between a brother and sister, or between a father and daughter, for example—was strictly forbidden and even punishable by death. The rules and regulations about family relationships could be extremely complex. But once the Indians were satisfied that a couple had a right to be married, the families conducted their customary business dealings to seal the marriage promises.

The men usually did the hunting and fishing, while the women built the houses—tipis, hogans, or huts—raised children, cooked for the family, and made clothes, tools, and utensils for the household.

Some tribes practiced polygamy. About half of all marriages of the Blackfeet tribe were polygamous, because so many men were killed in battle that the women outnumbered men by nearly three to one. Occasionally, although very rarely, the women in some tribes had two husbands. More often a husband had two or more wives, and sometimes the wives were sisters or other close relatives. If a woman was widowed, her husband's brother was supposed to marry her, whether he was married already or not. In a non-polygamous tribe or marriage, if a woman died, the widower was sometimes expected to marry a sister of his late wife.

Even among people who practiced polygamy, not all the marriages were polygamous. Many were monogamous. Arrangements depended on what a husband could afford—in particular, how many wives and children he could feed. In some cases only the chief was polygamous. Powhatan, for example, had many wives.

Native American families were often, though not exclusively, matrilineal; the property was passed down through the women. If a woman wanted to divorce a man, she could do so rather easily by dropping his possessions outside the door. There were variations on the divorce rites, including child custody traditions.

A Navajo legend, that was passed down from ancient days, recounted the story of a man and woman who had fought about sex. The man claimed that the woman was too interested in sex. As a result of the quarrel, all the men took their rafts and moved across the river, where they destroyed their rafts. Living separately, both the men and women suffered the tortures of the damned. Foremost, they were dying out. So the women asked the men to return. When they did, the men and women agreed that the man should lead the way about sexual matters, since men were the stronger gender. But they absolutely needed each other for survival in many ways. They complemented each other, and, realizing they were unable to exist without each other, they achieved a level of equality, with neither women nor men living in slavery or subservience to the other.

Women were never considered to be the property or chattel of men. An abused Blackfeet wife could go back to her own family, whether her husband objected or not.

Native Courtship

Traditional Indians tended to marry young. Often girls married soon after they began to menstruate or married a few years later. Different tribes dealt with their young, marriageable females in a variety of ways. Most encouraged some separation of the sexes—and sometimes very strict separation—until marriage.

Dances and ceremonies, sometimes only once a year, were opportunities where young men and women could meet to choose their mates. The young people weren't supposed to talk much with each other at such events.

The majority didn't place impossible demands on their adolescents. Young couples found many ways to arrange clandestine meetings. In hunting and gathering tribes, the women were expected to fetch water and firewood. When the girls went to the springs, streams, or the woods around their camps, young men arranged to meet or at least see the one they loved. Lovers also found berry picking times ideal for rendezvous away from the watchful eyes of older people. Flute music, in particular, was considered seductive, so young men composed and played tunes on their flutes for their lovers. When a girl heard a special tune, she knew her lover was nearby.

In certain communities, if a woman decided she wanted a particular man for her husband, she prepared a special type of food for him and invited him to a picnic. If he wasn't interested, he turned down the invitation, for he knew what was in the picnic basket.

A young woman, in some tribes, was expected to marry the first man she had sexual intercourse with; in others she was supposed to experiment sexually and gain experience. But in most cases a woman could expect retribution if she stole another woman's husband or committed adultery.

Young people could enjoy a variety of traditional, seductive courtship rites. The Navajo held a dance, which was, in a sense, akin to a debutante ball, where parents showed off their marriageable daughters. Young men appeared with their best horses or wagons, and girls bedecked themselves with jewelry—fertility symbols, such as squash blossom necklaces, in some cases, and beads, shells, and feathers in their hair—and clothes they had made or borrowed for the occasion. Navajo girls could choose their own dance partners and expect the young men to give presents. The women could be very bold, if they chose, to the extent that they might even lead a boy off into the bushes. Some Navajo parents didn't let their daughters attend the dances, because of their free-wheeling nature. But in general the Navajo were open-minded about premarital sex.

When young women started menstruating, they got plenty of advice about courtship and marriage from their older, female relatives. They found ways to put the counsel to good use when they spent their days tending sheep—and had clandestine meetings with their boyfriends.

Many tribes had a tradition called "nightcrawling" or "tipi creeping." A young man would wait until a village fell silent; then he would creep into his beloved's lodge or tipi and stay with her all night. At daybreak he crept away and returned to his own home. In some tribes, the man simply slipped his hand under a tipi and held on to his beloved. If the woman didn't accept the man, she might scream, and he could be caught and punished. Sometimes parents built shelves above their beds and made their daughters sleep there. That stopped the young men from nightcrawling successfully.

While nightcrawling was a general practice, different tribes had sharply divergent opinions about it. The Hopis accepted it as normal. But the strict Apaches thought it was dishonorable, and if they caught a man in the act, they might beat him and destroy his property. Some tribes absolutely forbade any socializing between girls and boys at all until they were married.

Where young people were segregated by gender, the psychological transition for newlyweds was difficult. Adults devised many ways to help young couples adapt to married life. Some couples spent a year living with their parents, often the bride's parents, before setting up their own lodge. Sometimes a bridegroom worked for his wife's family for a period of time and even lived with them before the couple began to have sexual relations. Some couples didn't live together, but each stayed with his or her own family until they had children of their own to raise. In some communities, a bride-groom, though expected to be respectful, wasn't allowed to look directly at his mother-in-law or have any contact with her except in dire emergencies. The reasons for that custom are complex, but it often helped young couples achieve a degree of domestic harmony and peace without interference from older people.

Girls learned to make their own clothes for weddings and other occasions. In the Southwest, however, older male relatives wove wedding dresses for the brides. The brides often kept the dresses to serve as their burial robes, too. Hopi brides had two dresses prepared for their weddings—one for the wedding day, and another for their burial.

Their husbands were supposed to hunt and supply the food. In the case of the warring Western tribes, where the men put themselves at great risk and often died during the hunt or in battle, their widowed wives married many times. Unless the widows were very young, however, subsequent weddings never entailed all the mighty preparations of their first marriages. Spinsters were virtually unheard of.

—::—

Bringing old traditions into contemporary life

Young couples want their families to get to know and like each other, to celebrate their joys together, and to comfort each other in difficult times. But once a couple decides to get married, it's a very good idea for them to keep in mind how people believed that young couples found peace and harmony if they kept a certain distance from their parents.

Remember to think for yourselves and not simply adopt the ideas of your parents, no matter how much you love them or how well-meaning you know them to be. Couples must live independent lives together as new families with their own standards, hopes, and goals.

Couple from Big Bend area of Crow Creek Reservation, 1890.
Photo by Father Ambrose Mattingly. Courtesy American Indian
Culture Research Center, Marvin, South Dakota.

*L*ITERATURE: LOVE POEMS AND FOLKLORE

*T*here is a wealth of fascinating and beautiful Native American literature that has been passed down and collected through centuries past. Here are some love poems that provide a glimpse of the profound longing and romantic feelings of young lovers, the conditions under which they lived, and the traditions that ruled their lives. While these poems shed light on courtship and marriage-related practices, they also make it clear that the Indigenous people of this land had the same universally complex relationships that all lovers have had, whether from ancient Egypt or contemporary Paris.

Indian poems had their roots in the songs and chants of tribal life. The Indians sang and wrote songs for practical purposes, to conquer or at least deal with the invisible forces in their lives. Songs inspired The People to conduct their lives honorably and helped them through times of great emotion and need.

A scholar named F. W. Hodge made this observation: "Most Indian rituals can be classed as poetry. [The poems] always relate to serious subjects and are expressed in dignified language, and the words chosen to clothe the thought generally make rhythm . . . The

A loving couple in an old print (www.clipart.com)

picturesque quality of Indian speech lends itself to poetic conceits and expressions. The few words of a song will portray a cosmic belief, present the mystery of death, or evoke the memory of joy or grief. To him the terse words project the thought or emotion from the background of his tribal life and experience, and make a song vibrant with poetic meaning. Many of the rites observed among the natives from the Arctic Ocean to the Gulf of Mexico are highly poetic in their significance, symbolism, and ceremonial movements; the rituals and accompanying acts, the songs whose rhythm is accentuated by the waving of feathered emblems, the postures and marches, and the altar decorations combine to make up dramas of deep significance, replete with poetic thought and expression."[1]

Songs were invented with a strong purpose clearly in mind—to compel love, express simple joy and a spirit of fun, praise the spirits and ask for help, explain life and history, express feelings about enemies and oneself, to quiet children, accompany work, or enliven games. The songs dealt with the many diverse activities and ideas that were part of daily life.

The following selections from *American Indian Love Lyrics and Other Verse*[2] suggest how elusive opportunities were for young lovers to meet, the shyness of the young girls, and the yearning for romantic encounters. This one reflects the boy's point of view.

HER SHADOW
(from the Ojibwa)

Out on the lake my canoe is gliding,
Paddle dipping soft lest she should take alarm;
Ah, hey-ah hey-ah ho, hey-ah hey-ah ho, thus I go!
Somewhere along shore she is hiding,
She is shy to yield to love's alluring charm;
Ah, hey-ah hey-ah ho, hey-ah hey-ah, love will win, I know.
There is a shadow swiftly stealing!
Should it be her own, soon I will win the race:
Ah, hey-ah hey-ah ho, hey-ah hey-ah ho, I think it is!
Will she but turn, herself revealing,
I will shout aloud when-e'er I see her face.
Ah! hey-ah hey-ah ho, hey-ah hey-ah ho,
There she is!

A second selection reveals one way that young lovers found privacy. Sometimes a young woman sat outside her family's tipi or lodgings and entertained her boyfriend under a blanket that hid the couple from the prying eyes of their families and neighbors. Sometimes, too, young women entertained more than one young man this way, one after the other, during the days when the youngsters were getting to know each other and preparing to choose mates. This poem also expresses the boy's outlook.

LOVER'S WOOING OR BLANKET SONG

(from the Zuni)

I.

O what happiness!
How delightful,
When together we
'Neath one blanket walk.
We together,
'Neath one blanket walk,
We together,
'Neath one blanket walk,
We walk.
O! What happiness!
How delightful,
When together we
'Neath one blanket walk.
We together,
'Neath one blanket walk,
We together,
'Neath one blanket walk.
We walk.

II.

Can it be that
My young maiden fair
Sits awaiting,
All alone tonight?
Is she waiting
For me only?
Is she waiting
For me only?

III.

May I hope it is
My young maiden
Sitting all alone
And awaiting me;
Will she come then?
Will she walk with me?
'Neath one blanket
We together be,
We—we two, we two,
We two, we two
Will she come?

The third and fourth selections express the girl's emotional outlook.

LOVE SONG

(from the Dakota)

Many are the youths, many youths:
Thou alone art he who pleaseth me.
Over all I love thee.
Long shall be the years of parting!

—::—

THE BRIDE'S SONG

(from the Algonquin)

There are many men in the world,
But only one is dear to me.
He is good and brave and strong.
He swore to love none but me;
He has forgotten me.
It was an evil spirit that changed him,
But I will love none but him.

Both of the last two selections are poignant songs. Does "Love Song" suggest that the young woman will not be marrying the man she loves and will spend all her life missing him? For a variety of reasons, it sometimes happened that young women didn't marry the men they favored most. Sometimes a girl's family vetoed a girl's selection and asked her to look further for a husband. That is just one possibility about the inspiration for this lament.

"The Bride's Song" suggests that the woman may have lost her husband's affection because he has succumbed to magic potions or herbs. This lament doesn't mean that the woman has lost the love of her husband forever; she might use a potion herself and woo him back. Sometimes potions and the havoc they wreaked in the lives of lovers were simply part of the courtship game, and true love could win out.

The following two poems are filled with the complexities of the authors' love lives, and are found in Frances Densmore's collections, *Poems from Sioux and Chippewa Songs* and *Chippewa Music*.[3] Densmore, a piano teacher and church organist, began visiting the Chippewa and Sioux during her vacations, and she started notating the songs she heard. She went on to prepare many publications and became a highly regarded collector, translator, and authoritative commentator about Native American poetry.

I SIT HERE THINKING OF HER

I sit here thinking of her;
I am sad as I think of her.
Come, I beseech you, let us sing,
Why are you offended?
I do not care for you any more;
Someone else is in my thoughts.
You desire vainly that I seek you;
The reason is, I come to see your younger sister.
Come, let us drink.

—::—

I AM ARRAYED LIKE THE ROSES

What are you saying to me?
I am arrayed like the roses
And beautiful as they.

I can charm the man.
He is completely fascinated by me
In the center of the earth
Wherever he may be or under the earth.

The first poem clearly addresses one man's change of heart. It might also be interpreted to suggest that one man, marrying sisters, finds he favors the younger sister—certainly not a situation that would promote domestic harmony in a polygamous marriage.

The second poem suggests that a woman may have used a love potion to charm a man. A wide variety of magic talismans have been used to guide the course of a person's life, but there was some unease about love charms, since they were used to gain control over other people. But to the contemporary reader, this poem can be interpreted as a straightforward boast of self–confidence by a woman happily in love with a man who, she knows, loves her. It would be an ideal poem to work into a contemporary marriage ceremony. So would the following poem from *American Indian Poetry: An Anthology of Songs and Chants* by Erdoes and Ortiz.[4]

THE HEART'S FRIEND
(*Shoshone love song*)

Fair is the white star of twilight,
And the sky clearer
At the day's end;
But she is fairer, and she is dearer,
She, my heart's friend!
Fair is the white star of twilight,
    and the moon roving to the sky's end;
But she is fairer, better worth loving,
She, my heart's friend.

Native American legends and myths have existed for thousands of years and are still relevant today. Many stories are moral tales about humankind's relationship with the natural world, as well as moving and poetic tales about love and the ritual of courtship. Here are two love stories from a wonderfully diverse and comprehensive anthology that readers interested in Native American tradition should not miss, *American Indian Myths and Legends*.[5]

—::—

THE LEGEND OF THE FLUTE
(from the Brule Sioux)

Well, you know our flutes; you've heard their sound and seen how beautifully they are made. That flute of ours, the *siyotanka*, is for only one kind of music—love music. In the old days the men would sit by themselves, maybe lean hidden, unseen, against a tree in the dark of night. They would make up their own special tunes, their courting songs.

We Indians are shy. Even if he was a warrior who had already counted coup on an enemy, a young man might hardly screw up courage enough to talk to a nice-looking *winchinchala*—a girl he was in love with. Also, there was no place where a young man and girl could be alone inside the village. The family tipi was always crowded with people. And naturally, you couldn't just walk out of the village hand in hand with your girl, even if hand holding had been one of our customs, which it wasn't. Out there in the tall grass and sagebrush you could be gored by a buffalo, clawed by a grizzly, or tomahawked by a Pawnee, or you could run into the *Mila Hanska*, the Long Knives, namely the U.S. Cavalry.

The only chance you had to meet your *winchinchala* was to wait for her at daybreak when the women went to the river or brook with their skin bags to get water. When the girl you had your eye on finally came down the water trail, you popped up from behind some bush and stood so she could see you. And that was about all you could do to show her that you were interested—standing there grinning, looking at your moccasins, scratching your ear, maybe.

The *winchinchala* didn't do much either, except get red in the face, giggle, maybe throw a wild turnip at you. If she liked you, the only way she would let you know was to take her time filling her water bag and peek at you a few times over her shoulder.

So the flutes did the talking. At night, lying on her buffalo robe in her parents' tipi, the girl would hear that moaning, crying sound of the *siyotanka*. By the way it was played, she would know that it was her lover who was out there someplace. And if the elk medicine was very strong in him and her, maybe she would sneak out to follow that sound and meet him without anybody noticing it.

In shape the flute describes the long neck and head of a bird with an open beak. The sound comes out of the beak, and that's where the legend comes in, the legend of how the Lakota people acquired the flute.

Once many generations ago, the people had drums, gourd rattles, and bull-roarers, but no flutes. At that long-ago time a young man went out to hunt. Meat was scarce, and the people in his camp were hungry. He found the tracks of an elk and followed them for a long time. The elk, wise and swift, is the one who owns the love charm. If a man possesses elk medicine, the girl he likes can't help sleeping with him. He will also be a lucky hunter. This young man I'm talking about had no elk medicine.

After many hours he finally sighted his game. He was skilled with bow and arrows, and had a fine new bow and quiver full of straight, well-feathered, flint-tipped arrows. Yet the elk always managed to stay just out of range, leading him on and on. The young man was so intent on following his prey that he hardly noticed where he went.

When night came, he found himself deep inside a thick forest. The tracks had disappeared and so had the elk, and there was no moon. He realized that he was lost and that it was too dark to find his way out. Luckily he came upon a stream with cool, clear water. And he had been careful enough to bring a hide bag of *wasna*—dried meat pounded with berries and kidney fat—strong food that will keep a man going for a few days. After he had drunk and eaten, he rolled himself into his fur robe, propped his back against a tree, and tried to rest. But he couldn't sleep; the forest was full of strange noises, the cries of night animals, the hooting of owls, the groaning of trees in the wind. It was as if he heard these sounds for the first time.

Suddenly there was an entirely new sound, of a kind neither he nor anyone else had ever heard before. It was mournful and ghost-like. It made him afraid, so that he drew his robe tightly about himself and reached for his bow to make sure that it was properly strung. On the other hand, the sound was like a song, sad but beautiful, full of love, hope, and yearning. Then before he knew it, he was asleep. He dreamed that the bird called *wagnuka*, the redheaded woodpecker, appeared singing the strangely beautiful song and telling him: "Follow me and I will teach you."

When the hunter awoke, the sun was already high. On a branch of the tree against which he was leaning, he saw a redheaded wood-pecker. The bird flew away to another tree, and another, but never very far, looking back all the time at the young man as if to say: "Come on!" Then once more he heard that wonderful song, and his heart yearned to find the singer. Flying toward the sound, leading the hunter, the bird flitted through the leaves, while its bright red top made it easy to follow. At last it lighted on a cedar tree and began hammering on a branch, making a noise like the fast beating of a small drum. Suddenly there was a gust of wind, and again the hunter heard that beautiful sound right above him.

Then he discovered that the song came from the dead branch that the woodpecker was tapping with his beak. He realized also that it was the wind which made the sound as it whistled through the holes the bird had drilled.

"Kola, friend," said the hunter, "let me take this branch home. You can make yourself another."

He took the branch, a hollow piece of wood full of woodpecker holes that was about the length of his forearm. He walked back to his village bringing no meat, but happy all the same.

In his tipi the young man tried to make the branch sing for him. He blew on it, he waved it around; no sound came. It made him sad, he wanted so much to hear that wonderful new sound. He purified himself in the sweat lodge and climbed to the top of a lonely hill.

Chief Sinte-Galeshka (Spotted Tail) of the Dakota Brule, and his wife, 1872. Photograph courtesy National Anthropological Archives, Smithsonian Institution. (Opps Neg 03121)

There, resting with his back against a large rock, he fasted, going without food or water for four days and nights, crying for a vision which would tell him how to make the branch sing. In the middle of the fourth night, *wagnuka*, the bird with the bright-red top, appeared, saying, "Watch me," turning himself into a man, showing the hunter how to make the branch sing, saying again and again: "Watch this, now." And in his dream the young man watched and observed very carefully.

When he awoke, he found a cedar tree. He broke off a branch and, working many hours, hollowed it out with a bowstring drill, just as he had seen the woodpecker do in his dream. He whittled the branch into the shape of a bird with a long neck and an open beak. He painted the top of the bird's head with *washasha*, the sacred red color. He prayed. He smoked the branch up with incense of burning sage, cedar, and sweet grass. He fingered the holes as he had seen the man-bird do in his vision, meanwhile blowing softly into the mouthpiece. All at once there was the song, ghost-like and beautiful beyond words, drifting all the way to the village, where the people were astounded and joyful to hear it. With the help of the wind and the woodpecker, the young man had brought them the first flute.

In the village lived an *itanchan*—the big chief. The *itanchan* had a daughter who was beautiful but also very proud, and convinced that there was no young man good enough for her. Many had come courting, but she had sent them all away. Now, the hunter who had made the flute decided that she was just the woman for him. Thinking of her he composed a special song, and one night, standing behind a tall tree, he played it on his *siyotanka* in hopes that it might have a charm to make her love him.

All at once the *winchinchala* heard it. She was sitting in her father's tipi, eating buffalo-hump meat and tongue, feeling good. She wanted to stay there, in the tipi by the fire, but her feet wanted to go outside. She pulled back, but the feet pulled forward, and the feet won. Her head said, "Go slow, go slow!" but the feet said, "Faster, faster!" She saw the young man standing in the moonlight; she heard the flute. Her head said, "Don't go to him; he's poor." Her feet said, "Go, run!" and again the feet prevailed.

So they stood face to face. The girl's head told her to be silent, but the feet told her to speak, and speak she did, saying: "*Koshkalaka*, young man, I am yours altogether." So they lay down together, the young man and the *winchinchala*, under one blanket.

Later she told him: "*Koshkalaka*, warrior, I like you. Let your parents send a gift to my father, the chief. No matter how small, it will be accepted. Let your father speak for you to my father. Do it soon! Do it now!"

And so the two fathers quickly agreed to the wishes of their children. The proud *winchinchala* became the hunter's wife, and he himself became a great chief. All the other young men had heard and seen. Soon they too began to whittle cedar branches into the shape of birds' heads with long necks and open beaks. The beautiful love music traveled from tribe to tribe, and made young girls' feet go where they shouldn't. And that's how the flute was brought to the people, thanks to the cedar, the woodpecker, and this young man, who shot no elk, but knew how to listen.

—::—

THE SERPENT OF THE SEA
(from the Zuni)

"Let us abide with the ancients tonight!" exclaims the elder.

"Be it well," reply the listeners.

In the times of our forefathers there was a village under Thunder Mountain called Home of the Eagles. It is now in ruins: the roofs gone, the ladders decayed, the hearths cold. But when it was alive, it was the home of a beautiful maiden, the daughter of the priest. Though beautiful, she had one strange trait: she could not endure the slightest speck of dust or dirt upon her clothes or person.

A sacred spring of water lay at the foot of the terrace on which the town stood. Now we call it the Pool of the Apaches, but then it was sacred to Kolowissi, the Serpent of the Sea. Washing her clothes and bathing herself over and over, the maiden spent almost all her time at this spring. The defilement of his waters, their contamination by the dirt of her apparel and the dun of her person, angered Kolowissi. He devised a plan to punish her.

When the maiden next came to the spring, she was startled to find a smiling baby boy gurgling and splashing in the water. Of course it was the Sea Serpent who, like the other gods, can assume any form at his pleasure. The girl looked all around—north, south, east, and west—but saw no trace of a person who might have left the beautiful child. "Whose can it be?" she wondered. "Only a cruel mother would leave her baby here to die!"

The maiden talked softly to the child, took him in her arms, and carried him up the hill to her house. There she brought him into her room, where she lived apart from her family because of her loathing of dust and dirt. As she played with him, laughing at his pranks and smiling into his face, he answered her in a baby fashion with coos and smiles of his own.

Meanwhile her younger sisters had prepared the evening meal and were waiting for her. "Where can she be?" they asked.

"Probably at the spring, as usual!" said their father. "Run down and call her."

But the youngest sister could not find her at the spring, so she came home and climbed to the maiden's private room at the top of the house. And there the maiden was, sitting on the floor and playing with the beautiful baby.

On hearing this the father was silent and thoughtful, for he knew that the waters of the spring were sacred. When the rest of the family started to climb the ladder to see the child, he called them back.

"Do you suppose any real mother would leave her baby in a spring?" he said. "This is not as simple as it seems." And since the maiden would not leave the child, they ate without her.

Upstairs the baby began to yawn. Growing drowsy herself, the girl put him on the bed and fell asleep beside him.

The maiden's sleep was real, the baby's a pretense. He lay quietly and began to lengthen, drawing himself out, extending longer and longer. Slowly the Serpent of the Sea appeared, like a nightmare come true. He was so huge that he had to coil himself round and round the room, filling it with scaly, gleaming circles. Placing his enormous head near the maiden's, Kolowissi surrounded her with his coils and finally took his own tail into his mouth.

So the night passed. In the morning when breakfast was ready and the oldest sister had not come down, the others grew impatient.

"Now that she has a child, nothing else matters to her," the old man said. "A baby is enough to absorb any woman's attention."

But the smallest sister climbed up to the room and called her. Receiving no answer, she pushed the door, first gently and then with all her might. She could not move it and began to be frightened. Running to the skyhole over the room where the others were sitting, she cried for help.

Everyone except the father rushed up, and pushing together, cracked the door just enough to catch a glimpse of the serpent's great scales. Then they screamed and ran back down.

The father, priest and sage that he was, told them quietly, "I expected as much. I thought it was impossible for a woman to be so foolish as to leave her child in a spring. But it's not impossible, it seems, for another woman to be so foolish as to take such a child to her bosom."

Climbing up to her room, he pushed against the door and called, "Oh Kolowissi, it is I who speak to you—I, your priest. I pray you, let my child come to me again, and I will make atonement for her errors. She is yours; but let her return to us once more."

Hearing this, the Serpent of the Sea began to loosen his coils. The whole building, the whole village, shook violently, and everyone trembled with fear.

At last the maiden awoke and cried piteously for help. As the coils unwound, she was able to rise. The great serpent bent the folds of his body nearest the doorway so that they formed an arch for her to pass under. She was half stunned by the din of the monster's scales, which rasped against one another like the scraping of flints under the feet of a rapid runner.

Once clear of the writhing mass, the maiden was away like a deer. Tumbling down the ladder and into the room below, she threw herself on her mother's breast.

But the priest remained, praying to the serpent. He ended with: "It shall be as I have said; she is yours!"

He and the two warrior-priests of the town called together all the other priests in sacred council. Performing the solemn rites, they prepared plumes, prayer wands, and offerings of treasure. After four days of ceremonies, the old priest called his daughter and told her that she must give these offerings, together with the most precious of them all, herself, to the Serpent of the Sea. She must renounce her people and her home and dwell in the house of Kolowissi in the Waters of the World.

"Your deeds tell me," said her father, "that this has been your desire. For you brought this fate on yourself by using the sacred water for profane purposes."

The maiden wept and clung to her mother's neck. Then, shivering with terror, she left her childhood home. In the plaza they dressed her with earrings, bracelets, beads and other precious things. Amidst the lamentations of the people, they painted her cheeks with red spots as if for a dance. They made a road of sacred meal toward the distant spring known as the Doorway of the Serpent of the Sea. Four steps toward this spring they marked out sacred terraces on the ground at the west of the plaza. And when they finished the sacred road, the old priest, without one tear, told his daughter to walk out on it and call the serpent to come.

At once the door opened and the Serpent of the Sea descended from the maiden's room, where he had been waiting. Without using ladders, he lowered his head and breast down to the ground in great undulations. He placed his heavy head on the maiden's shoulder, and the priests said, "It is time."

Slowly, cowering beneath her burden, the maiden started toward the west. Whenever she staggered with fear and weariness and was about to wander from the path, the serpent gently pushed her onward and straightened her course.

They went toward the river trail and followed it, then crossed over the Mountain of the Red Paint, and still the serpent was not completely uncoiled from the maiden's room. Not until they were past the mountain did his tail emerge.

Suddenly Kolowissi drew himself together and began to assume a new shape. Before long his serpent form contracted and shortened until he lifted his head from the maiden's shoulder and stood up, a beautiful young man in sacred ceremonial dress! He slipped his serpent scales, now grown smaller, under his flowing mantle. In the snake's hoarse hiss he said: "Are you tired, girl?" She never replied, but plodded on with her eyes cast down.

In a gentler voice he said, "Are you weary, poor maiden?" rising taller, walking a little behind her, he wrapped his scales more closely in his blanket. He repeated in a still softer voice, "Are you weary, poor maiden?"

At first she dared not look around, though the voice sounded so changed, so kind. Yet she still felt the weight of the serpent's head on her shoulder, for she had become used to the heavy burden and could not tell that it had gone. At last, however, she turned and saw a splendid, brave young man, magnificently dressed.

"May I walk by your side?" he asked. "Why don't you speak?"

"I am filled with fear and shame," said she.

"Why? What do you fear?"

"I came away from my home with a terrifying creature, and he rested his head upon my shoulder, and even now I feel it there." She lifted her hand to the place where it had been, still fearing that she would find it.

"But I came all the way with you," said he, "and I saw no such creature."

She stopped and looked at him. "You came all the way? Then where has the serpent gone?"

He smiled and replied, "I know where he has gone."

"Ah, my friend, will he leave me alone now? Will he let me return to my people?"

"No, because he thinks too much of you."

"Where is he?"

"He is here," said the youth, smiling and placing his hand on his heart. "I am he."

"I don't believe it!" cried the maiden.

He drew the shriveled serpent scales out from under his mantle. "I am he, and I love you, beautiful maiden! Won't you come and stay with me? We will live and love one another not just now, but forever, in all the Waters of the World."

And as they journeyed on, the maiden quite forgot her sadness, and soon she forgot her home too. She followed her husband into the Doorway of the Serpent of the Sea and lived with him ever after.

—::—

Bringing folklore into a modern wedding ceremony

Y ou may find poems that you would like to include as part of your wedding ceremony. The poems could be read before or during the wedding ceremony. Certainly the last two poems (quoted on pages 24–25) have their refreshing charms.

I t may be nice to include some poetry at the end of the ceremony program, even if it is not read during the service. Some brides and grooms may choose to write their own vows, and traditional poetry could certainly be incorporated into the vows, or at least serve as an inspiration.

S ome couples may choose to recite the vows or poetry in the original language, and then read the English translation. This would definitely add a special touch to the ceremony by bringing a part of ancient cultural tradition into the modern wedding.

T hese poems are only a sampling of poems that have appeared in collections of Indian prose and poetry. Books of Indian poetry are available in most major bookstores around the country, and there should be a selection of poems in libraries at universities and through any academic or public library system.

The two folk tales included in this book are both charming love
stories. The first, "The Legend of the Flute," would be a
delightful piece to read before the ceremony begins. A couple
may choose to have a flutist perform some traditional music
right after the story is read to tie it in with the proceedings.

The second folk tale, "The Serpent of the Sea," is similar to the
Beauty and the Beast story, and as it ends with a happy
marriage, it may also be a good choice for reading either at
the wedding ceremony itself or earlier at a rehearsal dinner, or
at a family gathering that celebrates the couple's engagement.

There are several collections of Native American folklore and
legends available at libraries and bookstores. Brides and
grooms may want to do a little research to find stories from
their own heritage or region.

Beautiful poetry and traditional love stories would not only set a
Native American–inspired ceremony apart from the usual
ones, they would give brides and grooms a chance to share
the richness of their cultural heritage with guests.

NOTES

1. From A. Grove Day, *The Sky Clears: North American Indian Poetry*, (Lincoln, University of Nebraska Press, 1951).

2. *American Indian Love Lyrics and Other Verse*, selected by Nellie Barnes, (New York: The Macmillan Company, 1925).

3. *American Indian Prose and Poetry*, edited and introduced by Gloria Levitas, Frank Robert Vivelo, Jacqueline J. Vivelo (New York: G.R Putnam's Sons, 1974). This can be found in the reference library of the George Gustav Heye Center and the National Museum of the American Indian in New York City. The Heye Center has several collections of poems available only for reference work and also different collections of poems for sale in the bookstore. The poem "I Sit Here Thinking of Her" comes from Frances Densmore's collection, *Poems From Sioux and Chippewa Songs*, and "I Am Arrayed Like the Roses" comes from Densmore's collection, *Chippewa Music*.

4. *American Indian Poetry: An Anthology of Songs and Chants*, edited by George W. Cronyn (New York: Liveright Publishing Corp., 1934). Copyright renewed by George W. Cronyn, 1962.

5. *American Indian Myths and Legends*, selected and edited by Richard Erdoes and Alfonso Ortiz (New York: Pantheon Books, 1984).

INTRODUCTION TO TRIBAL WEDDING CUSTOMS

*E*very tribe—Eastern, Western, Southern or Northern—forbids incest, and a violation of this proscription was punishable by death. Therefore, obviously, a parent and child, or sisters and brothers, could not marry. Beyond that, there were great variations from tribe to tribe about what constituted incest. Some looked very favorably upon marriages between first cousins. Others forbade marriages between members of the same clan; a clan was regarded as a family. The complexities of clan membership are enormous. To this day there is respect for the relationships between people in the same clan, and even if the members of a clan are not second or third cousins, a marriage between them is considered unacceptable. It can be difficult for anyone outside of a particular tribe to understand clan rules and regulations. However the wedding traditions and rites of Native Americans, though they may differ from tribe to tribe, are both facinating and easy to understand.

The Hopis and Navajos, primarily Arizona and New Mexico, have many principles in common, though they differ in specific traditions about marriages. Both used to require that a groom pay a bride-price, and the bride's family also paid tribute to the groom's family with gifts of equal and sometimes even greater value. Most Native Americans have shared that custom; in some communities, the exchange of gifts constituted the entire wedding ceremony. Sometimes the contract was even simpler than that.

One Teton Sioux man named Fools Crow remembered July 4, 1916, as his surprise engagement and wedding day.[1] A very active individual who regularly competed as a jockey, racer, and dancer, he was working with a few racehorses and a relay team in Kyle, South Dakota. At dinnertime he was sitting with his family when a girl named Fannie, the youngest daughter of friends of his family, came to his camp. She told him that her family wanted to talk with him. So he left his dinner and followed her, unable to guess the reason for the invitation.

At her camp, her parents served him dinner. They also told him that Fannie had fallen in love and wanted to marry him, and her parents approved. Fools Crow didn't know what to say at first, but then replied that he would discuss the matter with his father. His father told him that he and Fannie's parents had already decided it was a very good idea.

Fools Crow thought it over, went back to get Fannie and a few of her possessions, and moved them to his camp. "As simply as that we were wed," he recounted to Thomas E. Mails in the book *Fools Crow*.[1] "I feel it was one of the best decisions of my life, for we had a wonderful marriage."

If the two families made any deal about property, Fools Crow never mentioned it. Quite possibly, the parents did make arrangements that were more complicated than he revealed, but if so, Fannie's and his parents took care of them, and Fools Crow seems never to have given them a second thought.

For some tribes, the arrangements were painstakingly worked out in steps that took a lot of time, primarily because they concerned property, possessions, and prestige. Both the Hopis and Navajos, as only two examples, are matrilineal, meaning that their property is passed down by the women. There are other tribes that are patrilineal. The distinction has been very important, particularly when it involves divorce—a common occurrence in many tribes. In matrilineal societies, the women retain all the property, and the children always stay with the mother or her family. Not only among the Hopis and Navajos, but among most Native Americans, the children of a divorced couple, or even of a widowed husband, remain with the mother's family.

Luckily, non-Indians don't need to understand the elaborate rules and regulations of family and clan relationships to enjoy many of the traditions of Native American weddings.

—::—

NOTE

1. Thomas E. Mails, *Fools Crow* (Lincoln: University of Nebraska Press, 1979). This book was based on interviews with Fools Crow in the 1970s.

WEDDING CUSTOMS:
THE HOPI

The Hopi of Arizona celebrate all types of milestones in life with very specific rites symbolizing the continuity of life. When couples were in the courting stage, if a Hopi boy wanted a girl to become his bride, he made a bundle for her—clothing and fine white buckskin moccasins—and left them on her doorstep. If she accepted them, she accepted him, too. A wedding involves both blood relatives and members of the family related by affinity or close relationships. All the relatives have certain tasks they're obliged to perform. Some require a great deal of time and effort. A Hopi wedding may take such a long while to prepare for that the couple may already have several children by the time the parents are married; they include the children in the wedding ceremony. It's so common for the couple to have children by the time they are actually married that there is even a prescribed way for the youngsters to be dressed for the celebration.

A Hopi wedding is a serious occasion for the relatives of the bride and groom. The bride is not supposed to smile when she wears the robes woven for her by the groom's uncles. In the Hopi tradition, the male relatives of the bridegroom create the bride's robes for her wedding day. Hopi men are the weavers. The rites of the wedding are supposed to be a rehearsal for, or an enactment of, the rest of the bride's life, even to the detail of a robe she carries for a later ceremony—her burial. (In some tribes, the bride is expected to keep her wedding dress for her burial gown, but Hopi brides get separate garments for their weddings and funerals.)

Even though a couple is not technically married until the wedding day, everyone treats the children as legitimate offspring and fully deserving members of the family. Their relatives keep them away from sunlight until they are about three weeks old, and then they are taken out to see the sunrise at dawn. At that time, the child's life officially begins, and he or she receives a name. In the days before a Hopi wedding takes place, the bride spends time (most sources say four days) grinding corn. She may do it in her mother-in-law's house, or she may do the grinding in the presence of other female relatives, who grind corn with her. Corn is a very significant part of the Hopis' lives, and for that matter, extremely important for most tribes historically. The Hopi attach significance to blue corn, for example. Traditional Hopi belief teaches that blue corn plays a part in their origins. Upon arriving in this world, the Hopi were offered corn of various colors, and their choice determined their destiny. They chose the short, blue ear of corn. Though it signified that their lives would be difficult, it also meant they would learn to survive and outlive all other people on this planet.

While the bride grinds corn inside the house, various relatives wage a battle outdoors. No one gets hurt, but the fight makes a mess. To get the fight started, the groom's paternal aunts arrive at the groom's house with buckets of mud. They're met by his maternal aunts, who also have buckets of mud. The bride's maternal and paternal aunts arrive, similarly armed. The aunts throw the mud at each other. (Notice that it's the aunts who start the mud slinging, not the uncles, in this matrilineal society.) One group insults the groom while the other group insults the bride. According to one source, the maternal aunts may capture the groom's father and cut his hair.[1] At the end of the fight, everyone is exhausted, filthy, and hungry, but they join together to enjoy a feast, and the bride and groom are supposed to live happily ever after. (Jill McManus, a jazz pianist and writer who lives in New York City, has spent a great deal of time with the Hopis in Arizona. She composed and recorded a highly praised jazz recording, "The Sounds of Hopi." McManus says the mud slinging hopefully allows the relatives to vent their aggressions and hostilities before the wedding and to exorcise any demons that might cast a pall over the couple's marriage.)

The day after the mud fight, the wedding takes place. The bride, followed by the groom (who carries a side of mutton, a popular meat in many Hopi feasts and ceremonies), along with the groom's relatives, form a procession that walks to the bride's mother's house. There everyone celebrates the marriage with a feast.

In the very beautiful book *Hopi*, by Susanne and Jake Page, photographs show a relative arranging a groom's mother's hair for the wedding day.[2] The bride of this couple already has a daughter—the child wears white deerskin moccasins and leggings, the traditional wedding clothes for a child, and she has her hair styled by relatives. All the people participating in the wedding have their faces dusted with cornmeal, which is considered sacred.

In this case, the wedding took place at the home of the bride's in-laws. The bride and her daughter both wore white cotton robes woven by the groom's uncles. (Cotton dresses have long been traditional among the Hopi, while other tribes wore clothes of other fabrics, particularly animal skins.) The bride's second robe for her burial is of cotton, too; she carries it rolled up in a mat woven of reeds. The wedding celebration includes spruce boughs and prayer feathers worked together as an offering.

Bringing Hopi traditions into a modern wedding

If the bride already has a daughter, or if she is inviting a young girl to be her flower girl, the bride may want to dress her for the ceremony in a white cotton gown and white doeskin moccasins with leggings. For other ideas about wedding party dresses, see the chapter about fashions, pages 109–116.

Traditional women wear their hair in prescribed ways at different times of their lives. For more about this, see the chapter on fashions. The bride or any women in the bridal party may want to adapt one of the traditional hairstyles for the wedding.

Corn is of special significance and the wedding dinner should include at least one very special corn-based dish. See the chapter about food, pages 95–108, for ideas and menus for wedding feasts.

—::—

NOTES

1. *The World of the American Indian* (Washington, DC: National Geographic Society, 1993).

2. Susanne Page and Jake Page, *Hopi* (New York: Abradale Press, Harry N. Abrams, Inc., 1992).

Wedding Customs: The Navajo

*S*usanne Page, who first began photographing the Navajo in Arizona and New Mexico in the 1960s, became especially involved in the life of one little Navajo girl and her family. When the girl was about eighteen years old, she decided to get married and invited Susanne to attend the ceremony and take photographs. The bride sent out invitations—not a common practice with Navajo weddings.

But wherever traditional weddings still take place, they are often mixed with the customs of the larger, American society. Traditional Indian weddings—rare events now—usually take place in communities that have not had their cultures eradicated (or at least extremely diluted) by Western culture. Most tribes consider themselves to be sovereign entities. Issues of sovereignty are at the forefront of Native American struggles to this day. Even so, many Indians have been marrying according to the traditions of the Christian churches and other sanctioned officiators.

Susanne arrived at the bride's house in Rough Rock, Arizona, the bride's "hometown," at 1:00, the time the wedding ceremony was scheduled. From there, Susanne traveled a good distance up a hill to the hogan where the wedding would actually take place. To get there, she walked in the direction of Black Mesa, a high formation of rock about 60 x 30 miles wide, a major feature of the land in northeastern Arizona. The hogan was decorated with balloons, which were the only hint of the coming ceremony. The bride didn't appear; she was busy getting dressed.

The ceremony didn't actually start for another three hours. Unlike Susanne, the other guests had expected the delay, and they began to trickle into the hogan during the afternoon. The groom's family arrived from the escarpment, Black Mesa, which, on its distant southern edge, is home to Hopi villages. Susanne discovered the wedding was scheduled to take place so late in the day because Navajo tradition dictates that the sun must reach a particular position in the western sky—specifically, at sundown—before the ceremony could start.

Inside the hogan, the groom headed south, following the path of the sun, walking left, and sat on the floor. His family sat by him to the north. One of the bride's uncles, a medicine man, together with a small procession of people, went to the hogan with a cup of water in hand. Another uncle and the bride's mother carried food. The bride walked with them, wearing her "moccasins, deerskin leggings, a white satin skirt, and a blouse, bedecked in what appeared to be all the family's turquoise jewelry—bracelets, squash blossom necklaces," writes Susanne Page in her book *Navajo*.[1] Squash blossom necklaces are traditional fertility symbols among the Hopi and other tribes. The bride also wore a colorful shawl that she had bought for the occasion.

"She carried a shallow basket woven of yucca in which there was a layer of cornmeal mush," Susanne also noted. When the procession neared the hogan, the bride's mother handed Susanne a tray of food and told her to lead the procession into the hogan. About fifty people had gathered there in the very warm room.

The bride sat on the groom's right; her family sat on her right. She set the basket with the cornmeal mush on the floor in front of

Native American Courtship & Marriage

the group. The guests had already put their gifts of food for the wedding feast and their private gifts for the couple on the floor, too.

The medicine man, the bride's uncle, kneeled in front of the couple and directed them to wash their hands in the cup of water he had brought. Then he took corn pollen from a pouch and made lines across the mush in the basket. The lines pointed in the four directions according to tradition. Some lines were drawn in white cornmeal and some in yellow cornmeal.

Speaking the Navajo language as he told the couple about the responsibilities of marriage, he changed the position of the pollen basket. Susanne later learned that the movement was supposed to turn the bride and groom's minds toward each other. The medicine man directed the couple to eat some of the pollen.

Susanne was then surprised to learn she was supposed to lead the couple in reciting the "white man's vows." Conjuring up wedding ceremony vows from memory, she squatted down, asked the couple to hold hands, and guided them. And the couple was married. Then the ceremony turned even more festive as everyone dined, while the couple opened their presents and made a fuss about how wonderful the wedding and the presents were. One of the bride's sisters made her first appearance at the wedding at this time; she wore such an elaborate hairdo that Susanne thought it looked like "a Burmese temple."

Susanne ended her account by saying the wedding was the last in a variety of ceremonies or rites that took place in a Navajo girl's life, such as the celebrations at her birth and for the advent of puberty.

Susanne had not witnessed the preliminaries to this wedding. In this case, because it was a modern marriage, the couple's families probably paid nothing vaguely resembling a bride-price, and certainly they wouldn't have negotiated about an exchange of horses or household goods in the old-fashioned way. For those negotiations, when Navajos lived strictly by the ancient customs, the two families would sit down together and negotiate the price. Horses and other such practical items often served as the price; they also were symbolic of the serious merging of the couple's families' assets.

Among the Navajo, the groom's payment was of major importance. It was shameful for a Navajo bride to marry without receiving a bride-price. The bride's family probably would have paid at least as great a tribute. That was the custom in most Native American communities. It was the duty and privilege of the bride's family to hold its head high, as it were, and assert equality for the bride and groom. To be paid for was honorable. When the price was right, the marriage got off to a bright start.

The price didn't guarantee that the marriage would last. But the price did guarantee that the women had respectable standing and primary rights to the couple's property and children.

—::—

Bringing Navajo traditions into a modern wedding

To add a touch of traditions thousands of years old among the Navajo, a modern bride and groom can elect to have at the altar a small, very tightly woven yucca basket or plate filled with cornmeal mush, with white and yellow cornmeal lines crossing it, depicting the four directions. The Franciscan Fathers published a book, *An Ethnology Dictionary of the Navajo Language*,[2] fully explaining the cornmeal-in-a basket rite.

The basket, which was usually woven of yucca braid, had to be new. In the traditional marriage ceremony, a relative of the bride drew lines in the cornmeal mush with white and yellow cornmeal, and then drew a circle with yellow cornmeal around the whole, beginning and ending at the line with its end pointing to the east. After the hand washing ceremony of the bride and groom, the relative in charge of the basket turned it to have the east end of the line facing the couple. The bridegroom took a pinch of the cornmeal mush with his fingers and ate it, and then the bride dipped her fingers in at the same place and took a pinch to eat, too. The bride and groom did the same thing at the end of each line in the mush in the basket. That rite actually concluded the Navajo wedding ceremony.

The couple passed the cornmeal mush around to all the guests. Whoever ate the last bit of the cornmeal might take possession of the basket. Sometimes the basket was simply given to the bride's mother, who was not present at the wedding in the old days; she and her son-in-law weren't supposed to look at each other, according to a tradition now long gone. Or sometimes the basket went to the groom's family, and the person who drove the horses that were part of the bride gift consumed the last portion of the cornmeal. In traditional Navajo weddings, the conclusion of the basket ceremony signaled the start the of feast.

—::—

NOTES

1. Susanne Page and Jake Page, *Navajo* (New York: Harry N. Abrams Publishers, Inc., 1995).
2. *An Ethnology Dictionary of the Navajo Language* (St. Michaels, AZ: The Franciscan Fathers, 1910).

WEDDING CUSTOMS:

THE STORY OF AN EASTERN CHEROKEE BRIDE AND A MINNESOTA SIOUX BRIDEGROOM

*N*ikoa, a bride-to-be, comes from the matrilineal Eastern Cherokee in North Carolina. She belongs to her mother's clan, one of seven clans in her tribe. When she marries her fiancé, a Sioux from Minnesota, he will automatically become a member of her clan, and she will automatically become a member of his clan. Nobody else in either family becomes a member of the other's clan. So the bridegroom's brother could marry the bride's sister. But neither Nikoa nor her fiancé could marry anyone from their own clans. That would be incestuous. In the old days, Nikoa would have had to marry a Cherokee—but not someone from her clan. In those days, people didn't leave their reservations or, before the days of the reserves, their community. "We wouldn't have even met someone from another tribe," Nikoa explains.

Though she was raised as a Christian, she doesn't go to church. Her fiancé believes in the traditional religion of the Sioux. So the couple decided to get married in a traditional Sioux wedding ceremony in Minnehaha County, on the Shakopee reservation, about thirty minutes from Minneapolis, Minnesota. The bride didn't know what the ceremony would consist of, but she was going to wear the traditional clothes, whatever they were.

The couple will later decide which clan to register their children in. They could be either Cherokee or Sioux; the couple will base their decision upon land benefits and federally provided health care benefits, whatever will be most profitable for the child.

Though no one in the bride's family has been married in a traditional Eastern Cherokee wedding ceremony, Nikoa knows what it used to consist of.

A wedding vase was filled with a liquid important to the tribe. The vase had two spigots. The groom drank from one spigot, and the bride from the other.[1] A blanket was tied around the couple. "Nobody ever had a divorce back then," Nikoa says, "and if someone wanted to get divorced and married again, the blanket was untied and put away." The husband or wife or both were free to marry other people. "The blanket was like the wedding band," says Nikoa, an employee at the American Indian Community House in New York City.

Cherokee Marriage Traditions

Myths of the Cherokee and Sacred Formulas of the Cherokees, by James Mooney,[2] tells of the ways that Cherokee marriages were arranged. Among nearly all Native Americans, with the exception of the Pueblo, the hopeful bridegroom first received the consent of the woman he wanted to marry. Then he gave presents to her parents as a kind of compensation for the loss of their daughter. The gift giving formalized the agreement between the man and woman. But if the parents felt the gifts were insufficient, they could refuse them, and the marriage didn't take place. The hopeful suitor usually asked a friend or the brother of the girl to act as a go-between to settle the bride-price with the parents.

Another source, *Weaving New Worlds: Southeastern Cherokee Women and Their Basketry*, by Sarah H. Hill,[3] recounts the custom of the suitor who, having received permission to marry a woman, lays a present of wood at the door of his beloved's house. She signaled her acceptance by making a fire with the wood and offering him food to eat. The trade confirmed the marriage. Then the man's family brought a great amount of wood to the woman, and her relatives prepared a feast for both sides of the family.

An observer of the Eastern Cherokee wedding customs in around the year 1700 noticed that a young man always went himself or sent a go-between to a girl's family to arrange a match. Elder brothers often acted as the go-betweens for both young women and hopeful suitors. The parents answered that they would think about requests for their daughters as brides, then discussed the matter with all their relatives. Even the tribe's leader might give his opinion. If they approved, and if the young woman accepted the match, the suitor paid a bride-price to her parents. (The better looking the girl, the higher the price.) In any case, the marriage took place only if the prospective bride approved of it. A woman was never married against her will.

Bringing Cherokee traditions into a modern wedding

A couple can drink wine or any liquid that they choose out of the same cup or glass (an ornate chalice would be very appropriate) during a wedding ceremony.

Even more picturesque and easy for all the guests to see, a couple can choose a blanket, perhaps an authentic Native American blanket or shawl, to wrap around themselves during the ceremony or just after the wedding officiator says that the groom and bride may kiss as husband and wife. The officiator or a member of the wedding party can tie a knot in the garment, and then it can be folded and left that way for the couple to keep.

—::—

NOTES

1. See the chapter on fashions for a mention of the small Hopi and Santa Clara wedding jugs (silver pottery) in the section "Books on Indian Jewelry," page 114. These miniature sculptures are available for sale.

2. James Mooney, *Myths of the Cherokee and Sacred Formulas of the Cherokees* (reprint, Nashville, TN: Charles and Randy Elder, 1982).

3. Sarah H. Hill, *Weaving New Worlds: Southeastern Cherokee Women and Their Basketry* (Chapel Hill: University of North Carolina Press, 1997).

WEDDING CUSTOMS: THE IROQUOIS

*A*mong the tribes that especially like to protect their privacy are the Iroquois, who are leery of being used and commercialized. As a general rule, they do not invite outsiders to observe the ways they conduct their daily lives or their ceremonies and celebrations. Nevertheless, a great deal has been written about their history from the point of view of non-Indian observers, much of it admiring, including commentaries about Iroquois family, clan, and tribal structure.

The Iroquois have always been a matrilineal society. Women didn't rule over men, they simply had certain powers that balanced the powers of men. They had areas of authority and stewardship as did men in other areas. Iroquois men were very respectful of all women, regardless of race.

The Iroquois absolutely prohibited marriages between men and women of the same clan, and to this day they stick to this tradition. Historically most marriages were monogamous. The welfare of the children was a concern of both parents, and that concern existed throughout the parents' life. Marriage arrangements for the children was one of the major areas of interest and authority of the women.

When a mother thought her son was ready to get married, she looked around for a suitable girl, then negotiated with the girl's mother. Sometimes the mothers consulted relatives, but decisions about the arrangement generally belonged to the mothers. As in other societies, on those rare occasions when a girl had been ready for marriage for a while and still had not attracted a suitor, the mother of the girl might initiate a marriage.

The wedding ceremony was simple. On the day after a marriage was announced, the bride, accompanied by her mother or maternal grandmother, went to the house of the groom's maternal grandmother and gave her some wedding cakes carried in a basket. The number of cakes varied, according to some sources, from five or six to as many as twenty-four. It depended upon how big the groom's family was. The offering of the cakes proved that the young woman's family approved of the marriage.

Iroquois sources suggest that if the prospective groom accepted the bread he accepted the idea of the marriage. If he left the bread untouched he rejected the idea. Others say his mother had to accept the cakes, unless there was a valid objection. If the cakes were left untouched on the doorstep the family of the prospective bride took the cakes away—and felt humiliated.

But if the marriage was to proceed, relatives and friends of the groom ate the cakes and then filled the empty basket with meat. They returned the basket to the girl's family, who ate the meat with their relatives. Then the two families met, and important men in the tribes made speeches, expressed happiness about the marriage, and gave the newlyweds advice about married life.

The couple had to follow many rules and go through a succession of rituals, although many of them are not well known or have not been confirmed outside of Iroquois society. A young man may have moved into his wife's family's house for a while, perhaps two years, and hunted and fished under the authority of his mother-in-law. He always offered her at least a portion, and sometimes all, of what he had caught. All the marriage customs revolved around the lifestyle and survival tactics of the Iroquois.

Anyone interested in studying Iroquois marriage and lifestyle practices can find materials in the reference library of the National Museum of the American Indian in New York City. One good book is *Iroquois Women: An Anthology*.[1]

—::—

Bringing Iroquois traditions into a modern wedding

Just before the wedding ceremony takes place, or just after the vows are exchanged, or at the start of the wedding reception, which is probably most convenient for all concerned, waiters can serve canapés simultaneously to both the bride's and groom's relatives and the guests. These might include fancy cakes, perhaps some sweet cornbread cakes, and small meat cakes. There's usually a big meal after the wedding ceremony, but that is pretty much true of any Iroquois gathering.

There is no specific historical documentation about Iroquois or other Indigenous customs regarding the serving of finger foods at the start of a wedding dinner. Therefore, the hosts may want to print little messages on accompanying napkins or in the program, stating that the cornbread cake and meat snacks were inspired by an old Iroquois tradition.

—::—

NOTES

1. *Iroquois Women: An Anthology*, edited by William Guy Spittal (Ontario: Iroqrafts, Ltd., Iroquois Publications, 1996).

Wedding Customs: Oglala Sioux

The courtship and wedding traditions of the Oglala Sioux fascinated the white settlers arriving in the Great Plains. Sometimes the Oglala Sioux men kidnapped or captured women from outside their tribe. The men also devised more peaceful alternatives for getting to the altar.

Occasionally a man dressed in his best clothing, painted his face in bright colors, and wore a courting robe. Then he walked back and forth in front of the door of the tipi where the woman he wanted to marry lived. She peered out, then came outside to watch him. He kept walking to and fro, inching closer to her, until he could touch her. For a moment, she might seem to struggle to get free. But then she calmed down. He took off his courting robe and wrapped it around the two of them. They stood together, looking out at the world, signaling that other men should stay away from the woman. She was no longer available, at least for the time being. The woman's family invited the man to sit with them, placing him beside the woman. If she smiled at him, she signaled that she was willing to accept him. But if she turned her back on him, she rejected him. If she accepted him, she gave him a drink of water and invited him to come back another time. When he returned, she offered him food that she had cooked. If she decided she wanted to be his wife, she made a present of a pair of moccasins, which she decorated herself. If he wanted to marry her, he put the moccasins on right away. Then the couple was formally engaged.

The man's eldest and closest relative visited the woman's family and negotiated a bride-price, usually six buffalo skins or their equal in value. A very hardworking and pleasant woman might fetch an even higher price. Negotiations could take place over a period of several meetings, complete with feasts for the couple and invited guests that included both family and friends.

The couple developed a more intimate relationship when the young man sat near her tipi during the evenings and played the flute music considered to be so seductive. The woman went to meet him. To support her, her girlfriends built little fires with cottonwood tree twigs as a symbolic way of chasing away disagreeable spirits that could cause arguments.

The bride's dowry usually consisted of a tipi, a pair of robes, a bone awl and sinew thread for the bride to use in sewing skins, a cooking utensil, an ax, and a knife. The tipi was especially important. It gave the young couple complete authority over their lives together. The couple might have a wedding before the bride offered her dowry, but the dowry had to be paid before the couple could be considered properly married.

For the wedding, the bride needed a dress of soft, tanned deer or antelope skin, with the bodice decorated with the teeth of dogs. Her leggings, which reached from the knee to the ankle, were made of soft, tanned skins and were decorated with porcupine quills and feathers arranged in prescribed designs. She also needed moccasins of soft tanned skins for the uppers, decorated with porcupine quills or brightly painted designs, and rawhide soles. The bride parted her hair in the middle, combed it with a porcupine tail, oiled it with animal fat, and braided it into two or three sections. The braids hung down her back until she was married, and then she wore them hanging down in front of her shoulders.

If she had been treated to a puberty ceremony, she painted a red stripe along the part in her hair. (See pages 69–84 to read more about puberty ceremonies.) If she had also been through an adoption ceremony, she wore another red stripe painted across her forehead. If she had participated in some sacred ceremony, she could have her hands painted red. If she was mourning someone, she could paint her face black.

When she was dressed and decorated in these ways, her fiancé brought the bride-price to her tipi. Usually he arrived with his family and friends, with the women carrying the food for the feast. The bride and her family and friends also prepared feast food. As soon as the bride-price was delivered, the bride took the man by the right hand, led him through the door of her tipi, and seated him in a place of honor, at the rear, opposite the door. She put a pair of moccasins on his feet, then sat in the woman's place in the tipi, at the right side of the fireplace in the center of the tipi. That constituted the wedding ceremony.

If the bride didn't have her own tipi and welcomed him to the place where she lived, the bride and groom were considered married, but they weren't counted as a family in the tribe's census. They had to behave in certain socially acceptable ways with her family, paying special deference to her relatives, until they had a tipi of their own. So the man and woman usually hurried to erect their own tipi as soon as they possibly could. The tipi always belonged to the wife.

When the couple had their own tipi, the man could take charge of the marriages of his wife's younger sisters. He might even marry the sisters, and he could approve or disapprove of them marrying other men. If he had more than one wife, he needed a tipi for each of them. But all the tipis counted as only one family unit. The first wife was always the predominant wife in the family.

Other protocols existed for families in which a man had more than one wife, but none of the subordinate wives had full-blown wedding ceremonies, except for a feast. Women captured from other tribes didn't have a feast in honor of their marriages. They were considered married when they had learned to speak the Sioux language well, and their proficiency was judged by Sioux women. Most marriages were monogamous, however, since there weren't usually enough women to provide more than one wife for each man. Furthermore, the men discovered they could live in greater peace and harmony with one woman than with two or more.

Though the men had quite a lot of authority over women and possessed some hereditary birthrights, the tribe was essentially matrilineal in terms of possessions. Parents jointly raised their children, even if they got divorced. After a boy reached puberty, he came under the authority of his father or his father's relatives. Until the daughters married, they stayed with their mothers. Family relationships were very complex. All kinds of rights and privileges depended upon the order of the birth of the children.

From a very early age, little girls were prepared for their role as adults. Sioux girls knew they were expected to grow up to be mothers and raise their families skillfully. They were supposed to value hard work and remain faithful to their husbands. (The usual causes of divorce were laziness and infidelity, and men divorced their wives by beating a drum at a public event and inviting other men to take the women.)

From the moment girls went through their first menstrual periods, they studied the arts of quill embroidery and moccasin making. The girls may have already learned those skills before, but from that time on, they studied harder and worked more diligently. They had to learn quill and beadwork, hide tanning, and excellent cooking techniques to prepare themselves to be good wives. Parents loved for daughters to help with household chores and take care of younger children.

Girls kept track of their achievements, putting colored dots on their scraping tools to record the number of tanned robes and tipis they made. The Sioux held contests where the young women exhibited their handiwork. Beautiful cradles were highly valued, as they brought fame and fortune to their makers. "A cradle was equal in value to one horse."[1]

Older women counseled young women about sex, and the lessons were enhanced by various social rituals. One was called a Buffalo Ceremony and another was the Ball-throwing Rite, "at which a shaman officiated, enlisting the aid of the supernaturals." Everyone attended. These ceremonies were tantamount to social debuts.

Young men had to strive to make themselves attractive and conquer competitors for the woman of their choice. The men brushed their hair, plucked their beards, used perfumed grease, and wore finely tanned robes, carefully quilled moccasins, and white shell earrings. Some men simply were more charming than others. Some used love potions and medicines to increase their sex drive, and they studied playing flutes and making romantic music.

Some flute players were so talented they could entice a woman to follow them and elope. When an elopement seemed to be in the offing, the parents of the young couple usually had the foresight to exchange their bride-price gifts in advance.

—::—

Bringing Oglala Sioux traditions into a modern wedding

As with most weddings, the food can be a great center of attraction. See the chapter on food (pages 95–108) for ideas about what to serve. For private gifts, the bride and groom can give each other authentic moccasins made of soft animal skins sporting traditional Oglala Sioux designs.

At a gathering prior to the wedding, a man can wrap a robe around himself and his prospective bride while they formally announce their engagement to friends.

—::—

NOTE

1. The information here about Oglala Sioux customs comes from the book *Lakota Society* by James R. Walker, edited by Raymond J. DeMallie (Lincoln: University of Nebraska Press, 1982). This is also corroborated in *The Sioux: Life and Customs of a Warrior Society* by Royal B. Hassrick (Norman: University of Oklahoma Press, 1964).

CELEBRATIONS OF PUBERTY

When young boys and especially girls became adolescents, tribes staged elaborate celebrations. So important was this milestone for girls that, to this day, those who have not been assimilated or lost their traditions completely still celebrate. For the girls, the rites of puberty began immediately when they started to menstruate. Rites and feasts that introduced them to womanhood often went on for at least four days, and sometimes for a whole month. The celebrations were like many parties in cultures celebrating the coming of age of an adolescent.

Cubans celebrate when a girl turns fifteen. In the Jewish religion, when the children turn thirteen, a bar or bat mitzvah (for boys and girls respectively) marks the advent of religious responsibility and duty. Wealthy society girls become debutantes at age eighteen; their parents present them at elegant parties as the latest eligible brides-to-be. In the cultures of American Indians, menarche, the start of menstruation, was considered such a major rite of passage that adolescent girls became the center of attention of their entire community during this happy time.

Afterward, the young women were regarded as eligible for marriage, and it was just a matter of time—a very short time in some tribes, up to several years in others—before they married. As one Sioux said about the way his people lived early in the twentieth century, "Old timers got kids married right away. They tell them, 'You're ready for marrying now. You've got to get married.'" His father was about thirty and his mother had just become a woman when they got married.

The rites of puberty and the courtship periods in the lives of young people had many festivities attached to them. Tribes staged not only feasts and elaborate, spiritually significant rituals for puberty, they also sponsored other social events such as dances for adolescents. At dances, eligible young women met eligible young men.

Youngsters also devised other ways to meet, flirt, court, and enjoy one another's company away from the prying eyes of the elders. Some tribes taught the young women that they had to remain virgins, or at least that they should be very careful to maintain an image of virginal behavior. Other tribes didn't ask their young women to uphold very strict standards, and the youngsters could enjoy love affairs rather openly, some of which culminated in marriage. Whether or not first love blossomed into marriage, the youngsters acquired experience that prepared them for mature relationships. Sometimes they lived with their parents long after the wedding gifts were exchanged. In other communities, couples waited until they had children before they built their own lodgings and lived together.

It was rare that extremely promiscuous behavior in young people was encouraged or that boys and girls were kept physically separated until their wedding day; however, those types of tribes did exist, too.

When it came to the rites of puberty, most tribes immediately immersed the girls in ceremonies that introduced them to their duties as women. With the advent of puberty, the girls started to learn to do many chores that would become their responsibilities as wives and mothers.

Until they married, girls always lived with their mother, or with their mother's or guardian's family. Boys lived with their mother until adolescence; then they went to live with their father, or a male relative or guardian, to learn the skills required of grown men. A Papago woman in the early twentieth century remembered how her father, the chief of a village in southern Arizona, commanded the young men to run very long distances, as if in training for manhood. Men provided the raw materials of survival—animals and fish, animal skins, and wood. But women faced the challenge of turning those materials into tipis and hogans, meals, clothes, moccasins, bags, baskets, blankets, shawls, and all kinds of implements and tools. Women were supposed to nurture their communities during day-to-day life and support and inspire them through times of crisis. It's no wonder that part of the celebration of menarche virtually consecrated the young virgins to their lives as mature working women.

An excerpt from the autobiography of Maria Chono, who grew up in the old traditions of the Papago in southern Arizona, conveys a taste of the celebrations that a young woman faced when she reached puberty. (In the 1990s, the Papago renamed themselves the Tohono O'odham.) She told chronicler Ruth Underhill the following:[1]

> When I was nearly as tall as my mother, that thing happened to me which happens to all our women though I do not know if it does to the Whites. I never saw any signs. It is called menses.
>
> Our mothers watch us, and so mine knew when it came to me. We always had the Little House ready, over behind our own house. It was made of some branches stuck in the ground and tied together at the top, with greasewood thrown over them to make it shady. There was no rain then,

for it was winter, but it was cold in that Little House. The door was just big enough to crawl through, like our house door, and there was room for you to lie down inside, but not to stand up. My mother made me a new bowl and drinking cup out of clay, and put them in that house. When my mother cooked food at the big house, she would come over and pour some in my bowl, but no meat and nothing with salt in it. My father sharpened a little stick for me to scratch my hair with, because if I touched it, it would fall out. I was so afraid to lose my nice long hair that I kept that stick in my mouth all the time. Even when I was asleep, I had it there.

It was a hard time for us girls, such as the men have when they are being purified. Only they give us more to eat, because we are women. And they do not let us sit still and wait for dreams. That is because we are women, too. Women must work.

They chose my father's cousin to take care of me. She was the most industrious woman we had, always running with the carrying basket. That old woman would come for me in the dark when morning-stands-up. "Come," she said, "Let's go for water over across the mountain. Let's go for fire-wood."

So we would run far, far across the flat land and up the mountain and bring the water back before daylight; that old woman would talk to me.

"Work hard. If you do not work hard now, you will be lazy all your life. Then no one will want to marry you. You will have to take some good for nothing man for a husband. But if you are industrious, we shall find you a good old man."

That is what we call our husbands: old man. But this woman did it out of modesty, too, so that I should not have young men in my mind. "When you have an old man," she said, "you will grind the corn for him and you will always have water there for him to drink. Never let him go without water. Never let him go without food. He will go to the house of someone else to eat and you will be disgraced."

I listened to her. Do you say that some girls might think of other things and not listen? But I wanted to be a good woman! And I have been. Ask anyone in our village if they ever saw me with idle hands. Or legs, either, when I was younger.

All the girls came around the Little House while that woman talked . . . [T]hey sat and listened and when she was tired of talking, they laughed and sang with me. And we played a game with little stones and a ball. We pick up the stones in different ways with one hand while we catch the ball in the other. Oh, we have good times at the Little House . . .

I had to stay four days. Everything goes by fours with our people, and Elder Brother arranged it that even this thing should be the same. No woman has trouble for more than four days. Then they gave me a bath just as they did to my father. Oh, it was cold in the winter time! I tell the girls who come of age in the summer they do not know what hardship is. The water even feels nice in summer.

My mother came in the dark of the morning with the water in a big new jar. The women had to run all day to get that water ready for me. I tried to get away but my mother caught me and made me kneel down. Then she dipped a gourd in the jar and poured that cold water down over my forehead.

"Hail!
I shall pour this over you.
You will be the one who endures cold.
You will think nothing of it."

It is true, I have never felt cold.

Then my mother washed my hair with soapweed fibers. That is the way women should always wash their hair and it will never grow gray. She cut it so it came just to my shoulders, for we women cannot have hair as long as the men; it would get in our way when we work. But we like to have it thick and shiny, and we know that everybody is noticing. There was quite a lapful that my mother cut off, and she saved it to make hair ropes for our carrying baskets. She had new clothes for me; two pieces of unbleached muslin, tied around my waist with a string. We did not know how to sew in those days ...

Then I could go back to our house, only still I had to use the stick for four days and I could not eat salt. And then they danced me. All that month they danced me, until the moon got back to the place where it had been at first. It is a big time when a girl comes of age; a happy time. All the people in the village knew that I had been to the Little House for the first time, so they come to our house and the singer for the maidens came first of all.

That singer was the Chief's Leg, the man I told you about. He knew all the songs, the ones that Elder Brother first sang when he used to go over the country, dancing all the maidens. That Leg was the man who danced every maiden in our village when she came of age. His wife danced opposite him ...

"Come out," said my father on that first night. "Now you must dance or the Leg will drag you out. He's mean!"

I did not want to dance; I was sleepy and I had run so far ... But Luis, the Leg, came into the house and took me by the arm. He always danced next to the maiden, with his arm over her shoulders and the rattle in his other hand. He and I were at one end of a long line of people and his wife at the end of a line opposite. There was first a boy and then a girl, all down the line, with their arms over each other's shoulder and the blankets held along at the back. I told you the boys always like that dance.

The lines went to and fro, toward each other, and they kept wheeling a little, till at last they had made a circle . . .

We had no fire; we kept warm dancing. After every four songs, Luis stopped, because his voice was hoarse. Then he let me go, and we girls went and sat together while the men smoked. How dark and cold it was then, with only one ember to light their cigarettes!

There were girls who did not come to sit with us and boys who did not sit with the men. How dark it was! Some mothers went looking for their girls in the night and some did not.

At midnight my mother brought jars of succotash. She had been cooking all day for this dance, and every day after that she cooked and ground corn and baked bread in the ashes. Every morning we gave gifts to Luis and his wife. My cut-off hair and dried beans and cooked food and the hand-woven cotton that I wore for a dress. And to the girlfriends who danced beside me, I gave my beads and my baskets because these people had suffered and endured sleeplessness with us.

We stopped dancing in the dark of the morning and then my mother said: "Come and get firewood. Do you want to grow up as a lazy woman?" So then I went out in the dark to pick up the dead branches and bring them back before I slept. It seemed I slept only an hour before they were saying: "Get up! Get water. Get wood. Grind the corn. If you sleep at this time you will be sleepy all your life."

Oh, I got thin in that time! We girls are like strips of yucca fibre after our coming of age is over. Always running, and mostly gruel and ash bread to eat, with no salt. And dancing every night from the time the sun sets up until morning-stands-up. I used to go to sleep on Luis' arm and he pinched my nose to wake me . . .

At last the moon had come around again and they gave me a bath. It was over. I looked like half of myself. All my clothes were gone. All our dried corn and beans were eaten up. But I was grown up. Now the medicine man could cleanse me and give me a name.

You have to be cleansed as soon as the month is over; you must not wait. A cousin of mine did that once. She meant to be cleansed but she just waited. I think, perhaps, she did not have anything to pay the medicine man. But while she waited, one of her brothers was chopping wood. Something fell on him like a hot coal and killed him. So I went the day after my bath.

My mother and I went to the house of the medicine man early in the morning, with a big basket my mother had made to pay him. He drew a circle on the ground and made me sit in it, cross-legged, with my back to the rising sun. In front of me he put a little dish. Then he walked away where we could not see him and took something out of a little deerskin bag. It was the clay that he carries to charm the evil away from women . . .

[To make the clay, the medicine man] grinds up the bone of a dead man and some owl feathers so that they are fine dust.

He put that clay in a tiny bowl in front before me, mixed with a little water. Then he walked up and down four times, facing the sun that was behind me. Every time he came up to me he blew over my head and dusted me off with . . . eagle feathers to brush away the evil. And every time he turned, he made a noise like an owl: hm. The fifth time, he took up the bowl of clay and stirred it around with a little owl feather that was standing in the center of it. Then he put the clay to my mouth. "Drink this up!" So I drank it all.

Then he marked me, the sacred marks that are put on the men who have got salt from the magic ocean; the marks that take away bad luck and bring you a good life. On my breasts, on my shoulders, my back, and my belly.

"Your name shall be cha-veela." I did not know before what name he was going to give me; neither did my parents. The medicine man names one from his dreams. Some of my friends had names that could be understood like Leaf Buds, Rustling Leaves, Windy Rainbow, Dawn Murmur. But I have never understood my name and he did not tell me.

After all that work, I did not menstruate again for a year!

Maria Chono's tale addresses only the rites of the Papago, and yet they also contain elements of many celebrations of puberty—the spiritual ceremonies, the isolation of the young women, the work ethic instilled in them from that time on, the dancing and the feasting, and the physical exercises and hurdles a girl must face to become a woman.

—::—

Among the Apaches, a girl's coming of age was cause for a jubilant celebration called the Sunrise Ceremony, with haircutting, singing, feasting, and dancing. As late as July 1989, a puberty ceremony took place at the Mescalero Apache Reservation and the Fort Sill Apache Tribal Complex. The Apaches, being very hospitable, welcome visitors to this sort of celebration—although like most tribes, the Apaches don't welcome observers into every aspect of their rites, whether for this celebration or others. Some things are kept secret, for The People like to maintain their privacy. Even so, the author of *Women of the Apache Nation*, Henrietta Stockel, tells of her experience at a puberty ceremony, to which she was invited.[2] On the reservation, passing by tall green pine trees and horses grazing, in a landscape dotted with tipis and tents, she traveled miles to an annual, group puberty ceremony. During the four days of the celebration, a rodeo was scheduled to take place.

"This rodeo is not like anything you've ever seen," said one old timer to a younger man in a conversation that the author overheard. "When the horn blows at the end of eight or ten seconds, the Apaches don't get off. They just hang on until they get thrown off or the animal quits. Apaches don't quit."

The author noticed the rodeo bleachers on this hot day and, even more fascinating, a young Apache girl, perhaps only three years old, leading a tall, sturdy stallion across a field. What the child lacked in height—she came up only to the horse's knees—she made up for with the self-confident way she handled the horse.

The puberty ceremony began the next morning with the men building a medicine tipi, a structure opening to the east. Unlike other tipis, this one had unpeeled lodge polls. Neither the branches nor the bark was removed, and so the poles served as symbols as well as framework supports. "Closer to the ground, Apache men piled varieties of brush up and down the lodge poles, curling pliable smaller boughs around larger branches, creating vertical thickets that rose and descended along the entire height of the framework. Limbs, twigs, tendrils, all things green and leafy, went into the construction of the [tipi] that would enclose the maidens during the ceremony," wrote Stockel.

The Apache women kept busy kneading dough and rounding it into tortillas, which they dropped into black cauldrons of bubbling, hot lard. The women used long forked sticks to manipulate the batter until it became brown, hard, traditional Apache fry bread. Some tribes add powdered sugar, cinnamon, or honey to the fry bread, but the Apaches eat it in its natural state.

Throughout the four days of the ceremony, the families of the Apache girls coming of age provide food, such as boiled meat, beans, fry bread, mesquite pudding, and coffee or Kool-Aid, three times a day for everyone free of charge. (Dancer Louis Mofsie, leader of the Thunderbird American Indian Dancers, a world famous troupe presenting authentic dances and songs of Native Americans, says the families of girls facing puberty rites always play host to guests.)

At 8:00 in the morning on the first day, four young girls appeared; they wore buckskin dresses with exquisite bead designs, and beaded moccasins. A big entourage of people—godmothers, godfathers, and sponsors—accompanied them. The girls crossed the ceremonial grounds, keeping their heads bowed and their hands folded in front of them. When they reached the medicine tipi, they kneeled on the greenery. Facing east, they received a blessing from the medicine men. Some portions of the rituals conducted inside the tent were kept secret from visitors' eyes, Stockel reported. But she knew that older women put pieces of buckskin on the ground. The girls lay face down on the skins. And the sponsors massaged the girls.

Set back up on their feet, the girls ran toward the east and "around a basket four times. After that, Apache woven baskets full of candy and other treasures, symbolizing abundance, were dumped over the maidens' heads." Then trucks filled with candy and fruit arrived. The girls' families had sent them. The drivers threw the treats to the people. Then the families of the maidens brought the feast food out in large pots and served it. Afterward everyone, including the maidens, took a break; they went to their families' tipis.

Next came a parade with floats; a beautiful young woman in an Apache beadwork tiara and traditional Apache dress rode in a long white limousine with flags flying above her. She was Miss Mescalero of 1989. A Navajo band dressed in white and turquoise satin marched and played music. A traditionally dressed Apache couple rode astride together on the young man's horse.

In the afternoon, the rodeo began on time, but the dancing contest was postponed and then canceled because of the terrible heat. The Navajo Nation band provided music. Dancing would take place at night, when the air would be cooler. At night, a fire was started, and an announcer told the people that they were about to witness a festive but holy occasion.

With the sound of tinkling bells heralding their approach, "four men with their chests and arms painted black with white designs appeared. Wearing fringed yellow buckskin skirts with jingles, and moccasins, they shuffled, single file, toward the fire. On their heads ... were magnificent headdresses ... In their hands they held short staffs painted with the symbols of a people long persecuted, yet vital, resilient, and rich in heritage." They pointed at the fire and danced around it; a clown followed them. The dancers made a sound. "To the uninitiated it might have sounded like an owl's hoot," wrote the author, "but the notes were nearly soprano and were more of a call to or from the spirit world than an earthly harmonic. As they returned toward the fire in unending rhythm, a few women wrapped in shawls began to dance on the grounds..." The clown kept frolicking, entertaining the crowd. Then the maidens were taken to the medicine tent, where a fire hole had been dug in the ground and a fire begun. They went through more rites of puberty as the night progressed.

Indigenous people throughout the country, including the Apaches, generally maintained very strict standards of behavior for menstruating women, who were supposedly at their most "powerful and dangerous" during that time. They were isolated in special housing, where the "negative force" of their blood would not over-whelm medicine, spoil crops, or incapacitate warriors. Before reen-tering society, they had to bathe. The same rules applied to women who had just delivered their babies. Women had no contact with men, crops, or weapons during these times.[3]

—::—

Among the Navajo, as with most Native Americans, the rites of passage when a girl becomes a woman, called the kinaalda,[4] are the most important in her life. Girls wear traditional clothes and get their hair cut to a length just below their ears. Elders groom a girl's hair with a special brush made of wheat. Every day at dawn, the girl must run toward the sun. Furthermore, on the first and last days of the celebration, an older woman in the tribe becomes a masseuse for the girl; the woman massages the girl's body with the aim of rid-ding it of its baby fat and childishness and imparting to it the strength of a woman's body.

On the last day of the celebration, family members cook an enor-mous corn cake sprinkled with cornmeal underground on hot rocks and serve it to guests. At the end of the ceremonies, which include the feasting, the young woman becomes the newest link in the long chain of ancestors that goes as far back to its First Woman.[5]

Paul Radin, an expert on the Winnebago in Wisconsin, has writ-ten that the Winnebagos had many traditions, such as puberty cus-toms, in common with other Native Americans.[6]

Beginning when they were five, boys and girls listened to lectures about the customs of the ancestors. When the children reached adolescence, they were required to fast. For boys, fasting was the only rite of puberty. But it could be a tough one, because the boys had their faces blackened with charcoal and went to spend a night on a hill. Sometimes they went alone, sometimes with friends. Then they were sent back to spend two nights, then three nights on the hill. The boys were supposed to repeat the ritual until they were blessed; they were supposed to pray nonstop for the blessing.

When they faced this test, they could take either bread or charcoal with them. But if they chose the bread, their parents became angry, threw them out of the house, and tossed the charcoal out with them. Radin learned from an unnamed source that the boys usually took the bread and ran away into the wilderness; they did it to spite their parents, even though the boys ran the risk of being killed or captured by enemies. Parents wanted their sons to choose the charcoal so they would feel especially miserable and pray very intensely for a blessing.

One old man reminisced for Radin about how he and a friend were sent out as boys to fast on a hill together. They couldn't stop laughing at how funny they looked with their faces blackened with charcoal. On their way home, they used their saliva to streak their faces so they would look as if they had been crying and suffering.

Young girls fasted when they began to menstruate and had to spend time in menstrual lodges. Women went to the lodges from their first menstrual periods until the last time they menstruated. Menstrual lodges stood close to the women's home lodges so their families could stay in touch with them. Sometimes a woman's lover visited the menstrual lodge and had a sexual tryst. Unwelcome men might try to visit the women, too, and their families tried to protect them. Radin's informant said that families especially wanted to guard their women against "ugly" men, who usually had love potions, which were very difficult, perhaps impossible, to fight against.

As soon as a young girl went through her first menstrual period, she was considered ready to be courted and married. Radin, hearing about menstrual period customs, thought it was very odd that women could meet their lovers in the menstrual lodges. But Winnebago women were protected only against the visits by unworthy men, Radin was told. The women may have been married to their visiting lovers, or may have simply been considered married after the visits, or else the couple married shortly after the woman left the menstrual lodge. Girls were definitely married soon after they reached puberty.

Usually parents arranged the marriages, and the children rarely protested. But if a child didn't want to marry a particular person, the parents didn't force the match. As with many other tribes, the Winnebagos had no wedding ceremony except for an exchange of gifts.

—::—

NOTES

1. *Native American Autobiography: An Anthology*, edited by Arnold Krupat (Madison: University of Wisconsin Press, 1994). This excerpt comes from chapter 18, "Autobiography of a Papago Woman," edited by Ruth Underhill, in part 5: "The Anthropologists' Indians, 1900. . ."

   The anthology notes that Maria Chono was the daughter of a Tucson chief in a village called Mesquite Root west of Tucson. She learned to weave baskets, as did all the Papago women. She also had an uncommonly independent spirit. The Papago were divided between Arizona and Mexico, and were primarily Catholic from their contacts with the Spanish, but they also retained beliefs in the teachings of their own, older faith. Ruth Underhill interviewed Maria Chono in the early 1930s. Underhill spoke a few words of Papago, and Chono knew some Spanish. Chono's account of her life depends heavily on the translation and interpretation of white people; her tale is essentially a composite.

2. H. Henrietta Stockel, *Women of the Apache Nation* (Reno: University of Nevada Press, 1991).

3. Sarah H. Hill, *Weaving New Worlds: Southeastern Cherokee Women and Their Basketry* (Chapel Hill: University of North Carolina Press, 1997).

4. For in-depth information about the Sunrise Ceremony and the kinaalda, as well as other female puberty rites, you can search online for "puberty rites," or visit Web sites for specific tribes.

5. Susanne Page and Jake Page, *Navajo* (New York: Harry N. Abrams Publishers, 1995).

6. Paul Radin, *The Winnebago Tribe* (Lincoln: University of Nebraska Press, 1990), originally published as part of the *Thirty-Seventh Annual Report of the Bureau of American Ethnology*, Smithsonian Institution, Washington, DC, 1923.

DANCES AND
POWWOWS

*L*ouis Mofsie, a Hopi-Winnebago by heritage, leader and founder of the Thunderbird American Indian Dancers, travels all over the United States, Israel, and Japan, dancing with his troupe gathered from many tribes. He wants to preserve the traditions and educate other people about the great artistic legacy and culture of Native Americans. Schedules of his group's spectacular, exciting performances done in authentic regalia are usually available from the American Indian Community House and the National Museum of the American Indian. Sometimes Mofsie's group dances at the Theater for the New City in New York City, among other performance spaces in Manhattan and throughout the Northeast.

Native Americans celebrate weddings with feasts, just as most everyone else does. There aren't any special dances for weddings. However, traditional Native Americans do have some special dances for the rites of puberty. One such dance is the "Mountain Spirit Dance," danced by the spirits of the four sacred mountains of the Apaches in Arizona, in a desert area surrounded by mountains. Information about the dance is available, listed under the "Mountain Spirit Dance of the Apaches," in books in stores, at the National

The Thunderbird American Indian Dancers, an internationally acclaimed dance troupe based out of New York City. Photograph courtesy Louis Mofsie.

Museum of the American Indian, online, and at many libraries, particularly libraries from universities with Native American studies courses.

Mofsie used to perform the Mountain Spirit Dance with his Thunderbird Dancers, but he no longer does because he has been advised by the Apaches that they want to keep it private. Not every tribe has dances or songs for its rites of puberty, but every tribe considers the rites themselves as a blessing.

However, there's one dance, called the round dance or circle dance (they're both the same), that everyone is welcome to witness and take part in these days. The circle dance was originally used to introduce young men and women when they reached adolescence. Young women held hands, and so did the young men, and they danced a simple, shuffle step in rings around each other. Ordinarily men and women didn't dance or sing together. Drums and rattles have provided most of the accompaniment for the singing and for the dancing, too—both usually performed only by the men. Young men played flutes as a melody instrument and for courting. Traditional Native Americans usually used music for rituals and ceremonies connected with religion, farming, hunting, fishing, warring, medical, puberty, and funeral rites, as well as other life cycle rituals. Women sang lullabies, and they had their own styles of dancing in their own social groups.

As an historic sidelight, Indian drumming definitely influenced jazz, though it is unknown to what degree. Many Native Americans and African-Americans intermarried, and in some ways the cultures blended. American Indian drumming techniques are believed to have had a great impact on African-American rhythmic techniques and innovations for jazz.

Powwows are among the best places to see Indian dances these days, hear the drums, watch The People compete and maintain traditions, while reaching out to communicate with and play host to non-Natives. Skilled artisans usually sell a variety of crafts. But for the original inhabitants of the United States, powwows are part ritual, part homecoming, and a reaffirmation of cultural identity. At powwows, Native Americans of many tribes gather to celebrate their cultures, confirm their identities, dance, feast, and greet old friends and make new ones.

If you are able to attend, you'll find yourself thrilling to the powerful sound of the powwow drums. The drumbeat pulls at everyone's pulse. You'll hear the chanting, too, and then see dancers in breathtaking regalia—furred, feathered, flashing with beadwork, and enhanced by face paint. According to the U.S. census, there are about 2.4 million self-identified Native Americans in the United States. About 1.4 million of these are tribally enrolled.

Hundreds of powwows are held annually all over the United States, and they take place year-round. Drums call New Englanders to the Fourth of July powwow held by the Wampanoags in

Mashpee, Massachusetts, on Cape Cod. They invite others to the lavish celebration at United Tribes Technical College in Bismarck, North Dakota, during late summer. Drums beckon many people to the large and splendid Oklahoma, New Mexico, and Montana powwows, and to the Labor Day powwow of the Shinnecocks on their reservation in Southampton, on Long Island, New York, which has become a nearly obligatory media event, since it's larger than most other powwows in the United States.

Tribes have different powwow traditions. For example, the Wampanoags of Massachusetts never used a drum until the twentieth century. The drums came from the Sioux, Pawnee, Omaha, and others in the Plains.

In the 1930s, many federal laws barring Native Americans from preserving their cultures were lifted. What's more, improved transportation made it easier for everyone to travel. Tribes visited each other's festivals. Now their dances, songs, customs, skills, and talents have formed a brimming pool of pan-Indian culture.

Tribes have centuries-old religious ceremonies, to which non-Indians are not invited. These include dances celebrating harvests and rainfalls, as well as, of course, the life passages for boys and girls arriving at adulthood and preparing for marriage. Non-Indians can see some of these dances in the repertory of the Thunderbirds. Some traditional dances have undergone a metamorphosis. In an attempt to preserve tribal cultures by presenting a united social front, Native Americans have evolved pan-Indian dances at powwows.

The gourd or grass dance, originally a war dance done only by Plainsmen dressed in elaborate regalia that included eagle feathers for headdresses and waist bustles, and blades of grass intertwined in the regalia, changed into an animated fancy dance. A circle, which women used to form around the dancing warriors, became the round dance or circle dance—a welcoming dance with everyone invited to join. The dance signifies the oneness of all people. "The forty-niners (round dances) are so popular, they often attract more people than the official powwows," Louis Mofsie has said with a smile, remembering his observations of dances and powwows across the country.

For non-Indians, powwows are educational entertainment as varied as the regions in which the tribes live. They can watch such things as the gourd dance to honor veterans. Native Americans have sent an impressive number of servicemen, most of them volunteers, to the country's wars—twelve thousand in World War I, before Indians had citizenship. More than double that number went to World War II, where the famous Navajo Code Talkers used the Navajo language as an unbreakable code to stymie the Japanese. "Indians were awarded seventy-one Air Medals, fifty-one Silver Stars, forty-seven Bronze Stars, thirty-four Distinguished Flying Crosses, and two Congressional Medals of Honor," wrote Arlene Hirschfelder in her prize-winning book, *Happily May I Walk*.[1]

One Sioux, who has competed as a dancer at Plains powwows, summed up his spirit, which blends modern goals with respect for the old ways: "I read of old warriors and their eagle feathers. They got themselves psyched up before they went into battle. I read where they danced in animal costumes to get the adrenaline flowing. They danced in a circle and never backed up, because a warrior never backs up."

—::—

Incorporating traditional dances and powwow customs into the wedding celebration

Some couples may choose to hire traditional dancers to perform at their wedding reception. Perhaps the bride and groom could do a little research and perform a traditional dance as their "first dance." Others in the wedding party, the bridesmaids and groomsmen, for example, may want to perform their own dances as well.

Another idea is to hire musicians or a band that specializes in Native American music and songs. Many guests may enjoy their first taste of traditional Native American music at a wedding. The information that follows will provide some resources.

POWWOWS

Here are a few notable powwows where people can go to observe and bring back ideas, crafts, and customs to add to their own engagement and wedding parties. In some cases, powwows charge an entrance fee.

Alaska: The World Eskimo-Indian Olympics are always held in Fairbanks during a weekend in July. Native Americans from the north compete in Arctic skills, sports, and dance contests. Phone: (907) 452-6646. Web site: http:www.weio.org.

—::—

Massachusetts: The Mashpee Wampanoag Powwow is held in Mashpee over the Fourth of July weekend and attracts Native Americans from all over the country. Visitors should sample the plum porridge served there. The powwow ends with a worship service and a clambake. Write Powwow, c/o Tribal Council, Mashpee, MA 02649. Phone: (508) 477-0208.

—::—

Montana: The Crow Fair, on the Crow reservation about 65 miles from Billings, attracts a big crowd to a parade, rodeo, dances, and a feast. For information, write or call the Crow Tribal Council, PO Box 159, Crow Agency, MT 59022. Phone: (406) 638-2601.

—::—

New Mexico: The Gathering of Nations Powwow takes place in April, with dozens of events and thousands of participants. Call or write the Gathering of Nations Information Office, c/o Box 75102, Station 14, Albuquerque, NM 87194. Phone: (505) 836-2810. Web site: www.gatheringofnations.com. You can also call the Albuquerque Conference and Visitors Bureau at (505) 842-9918.

The Gallup Ceremonial in Red Rock State Park is an outdoor event renowned for Southwestern crafts as well as for dancing and a rodeo. The event focuses primarily on the northern and southern Plains tribes, whose horsemanship is close to perfection, and features some of the finest riding and roping in the West. Contact the Intertribal Indian Ceremonial Association, 226 W. Cole Ave., Gallup, NM 87301. Phone: (505) 863-3896.

Other sources of information in New Mexico are The Indian Pueblo Cultural Center, phone: (800) 766-4405. Web site: www.indianpueblo.org, and the Visitors Bureau, phone: (800) 284-2282. Both are in Albuquerque.

New York Area (Long Island): The Shinnecock Powwow in Southampton over the Labor Day weekend. For exact dates, contact the American Indian Community House. Phone: (212) 598-0100. Web site: www.aich.org.

—::—

North Dakota: The United Tribes Powwow takes place in Bismarck on the Thursday–Sunday after Labor Day. This is a traditional Plains Indian celebration and ceremonial, complete with tipis and buffalo meat. The war bonnet originated in these parts and can be seen here in all its glory. Contact the United Tribes Technical College, 3315 University Drive, Bismarck, ND 58504. Phone: (701) 255-3285, ext. 1293, weekday afternoons between 1:00 and 5:00.

—::—

Oklahoma: Many powwows take place in this state on the weekends. The American Indian Exposition, featuring greyhound and horse races and a parade, takes place in Anadako in August. For information, contact the Chamber of Commerce, (405) 247-6652.

For other powwows in Oklahoma, call the various tribes: the Comanches in Elgin, (580) 492-3822; the Fort Sill Apache Tribe in Apache, (580) 588-2298; the Kiowas in Carnegie, (580) 654-2300; and the Wichita Tribe in Anadarko, (405) 247-2425.

Powwows are held for a variety of reasons; some are held by churches, schools, or individual families to honor a person and some are fundraisers. The Red Earth powwow/arts and crafts festival is usually held in June in Oklahoma City. You can contact the Chamber of Commerce at (405) 297-8900, or the Red Earth Festival at (405) 427-5228. Web site: www.redearth.org.

—::—

For a complete guide to powwows, consult the *Powwow Calendar*, listing over one-thousand powwows and Native American events by date and location in book form. Available through bookstores across the nation. *Powwow Calendar* can be ordered from Mail Order Catalog, PO Box 180, Summertown, TN 38483; phone: 800-695-2241.

Powwow Directory available as either a bimonthly newsletter or a biannual volume from Indian Country Communications, c/o Lac Courte Oreilles Reservation, 7831 N. Grindstone Avenue, Hayward, WI 54843. Phone: (715) 634-5226, Monday through Friday year-round. The newsletter has the advantage of including updates for powwows, which sometimes change their dates.

—::—

NOTES

1. Arlene Hirschfelder, *Happily May I Walk* (New York: Charles Scribner's Sons, 1987).

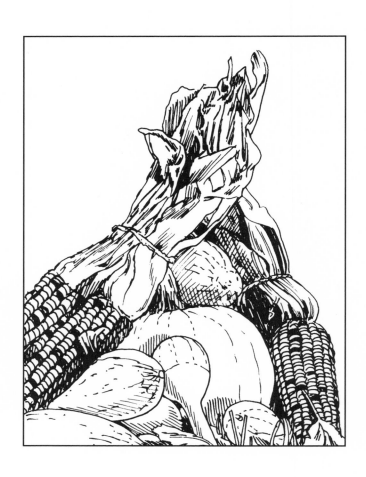

OOD

When planning meals for parties associated with engagements and weddings, recipes based on homey, earthy, traditional Native American foods can provide a lively alternative to more familiar cuisine. The original people of this continent were ingenious in their discovery and use of the nutritious and often tasty foods provided by nature in the wilderness of virtually every climate. Thousands of years before Christ, Indians began preparing wild corn and devising countless ways to cook and serve it as food, flavor enhancers, soups, and drinks.

Botanists digging in a cave in New Mexico in the twentieth century found ears of maize that they analyzed and believed were about five thousand years old. Then they found a newer form of cultivated, crossbred corn, which they believed originated around the year 1 AD. Long before white settlers came to North America, most Native Americans regarded corn as a staple of their diet.

They boiled, toasted, baked, fried, and roasted it. They mixed it with meat, fish, and vegetables that they both grew and found in the wild, plus fruits and nuts. They ground corn into flour for bread and cake, thickened soups with it, included it in stews, and invented corn porridge and succotash among other corn-based foods. The white settlers adopted some of these foods, most notably succotash, and corn bread. The saga of corn in the lives of the Native Americans probably began when traders brought wild corn from Central to North America.

Regional Cuisine

In the Pacific Northwest, Native Americans didn't rely upon corn, beans, or squash, as many tribes in the rest of the country did. In the Northwest, Native Americans dined on wild plants, roots, berries, and nuts, acorns in particular. These accompanied their primary diet of fish, especially salmon (which they prepared in many ways and stored in great quantities), shellfish, and small game. Although they weren't great fans of plants and vegetables, they did like a plant related to the hyacinth. With a nutritious, edible bulb, it became a staple of their diet. Seafood was important on the Gulf of Mexico and the East Coast, too—much more important than vegetables and plants.

Meat was an important source of protein in the traditional diet. There were few meals that didn't include some kind of meat. A balanced diet was valued. Many agricultural tribes served corn and beans, both of them secondary sources of protein, along with meat. They also knew to include starch, sugar, and fats in their meals and learned which plants, both wild and cultivated, contained the nutrients they needed.

Tribes in the Northwest regarded berries as important and had many ways of preparing them. Sometimes they cooked berries into a pulpy mass and dried them into cakes. Some tribes devised water-tight baskets for boiling. The Southwestern tribes were masterful basket makers. Many tribes placed food on top of hot stones buried in large, shallow pits, covered them with leaves and mats, and steamed the food by pouring water through to the stones.

Acorns were a staple food for the majority of the Indigenous Californians. They devised many ways of cooking and storing acorns; though some of the concoctions were tasteless, they provided nutrients.

Of all the wild animals the people of the Plains hunted, they valued the buffalo the most, for they could use every part of it, except its snout, for baking, boiling, and roasting. One Spanish explorer, writing about his first taste of buffalo (or bison) in the sixteenth century, thought it was a finer and fatter animal than cattle in his own country. Buffalo ranged from the Rockies in the west to the Allegheny Mountains in the east, and from Canada in the north to Mexico in the south. Of all the game available, deer, antelope, and elk were the animals of choice after the buffalo.

On the prairies of the Midwest and the Great Plains, Native Americans loved onions and turnips, which mixed easily with other foods and made them tastier. They also found them easy to store. Among other popular foods were strawberries, gooseberries, artichokes, cherries, and plums. Usually the older women and youngest girls did the berry, fruit, and vegetable picking. When they discovered an especially abundant cache of vegetables, whole families, including the men, joined in the harvesting.

Native Americans loved game birds, too. In season, particularly in the spring and fall, ducks, geese, and other birds migrated over the United States. Some tribes maintained flocks of domesticated turkeys, and there also were wild turkeys in the South and Southeast.

In the East, where people had a varied menu of fish, game, corn, wild fruits, and plants, they used mushrooms as a basis for bread baking. That was true all along the coast from New England to the

Deep South. New England tribes also tapped maple trees for the sap to make sugar and syrup.

In the Southwest, the Hopi discovered that mixing salty clay with some bitter foods made them edible. The Hopi also used cactus fruits and dried squash to enliven the taste of food and make up for a lack of sugar sources in their arid area.

From the corn soups of the Southern tribes to the tasty creations of the Plains tribes, simple and elegant soups as a first course would be a great way to introduce your guests to a Native American appetizer. It could very well be the most exotic soup ever served at an engagement or wedding party. Here are some recipe ideas.

—::—

HOMINY SOUP

From the Southern tribes.

¼ pound salt pork or bacon
1 onion, peeled and sliced
2 (1 pound, 13-ounce) cans hominy
1 quart buttermilk
½ teaspoon salt
Pepper
Chopped fresh parsley or chives, for garnish

Sauté the salt pork or bacon in a large stockpot over medium heat until cooked. Drain the fat.

Add the onion to the pot, and sauté until golden.

Stir in the hominy and continue to cook over medium-low heat, stirring occasionally, for 5 minutes.

Add the buttermilk, salt, and pepper to taste. Continue to cook over medium-low heat for an additional 5 minutes. Do not bring the soup to a simmer or it may curdle. Remove the salt pork or bacon before serving. Serve the soup warm, not hot, garnished with the chopped chives or parsley.

Makes 8–10 servings.

Dried Corn Soup

A variation of corn soup from the Plains Indians.

1 ear dried blue and white or yellow corn
   (remove kernels from the cob)
5 cups water
1 slice bacon
2½ ounces dried beef, finely chopped
Pepper

Soak the corn in 2 cups of water for 48 hours.

Place the corn and its soaking water in a large stockpot or saucepan. Add 5 additional cups of water and the bacon slice. Cover and simmer for 3½–4 hours or until the corn is tender but not soft.

Add the dried beef and pepper to taste and cook for 10 minutes more. Serve hot.

Makes 6 servings.

—::—

CONSOMMÉ OF TROUT

This elegant consommé is an alternative to a corn-based soup.

8 cooked trout heads
5 cups water
1 teaspoon salt
Pepper
2 tablespoons chopped fresh parsley, for garnish

Combine the trout heads, 5 cups water, salt, and pepper to taste in a stockpot. Simmer for 30 minutes.

Strain the soup and garnish with the parsley just before serving. This soup may also be served cold as an aspic.

Makes 4–6 servings.

The Apache obtained nourishing foods from wild plants, among them some cactus fruits, piñon nuts, bulbs and roots of many kinds, mesquite beans, mushrooms, greens, berries, acorns, and seeds.

Indians thought very highly of their diet and considered it superior to foods eaten by white people. As Maria Chono recalled, she began grinding seeds as a very young girl, and her mother made gruel out of wild seeds: "Wild seeds and cactus, those are the good foods," she said.[1]

Several cookbooks focus on Native American cooking. Presented in a very sophisticated, comprehensible way, *New Native American Cooking* by Dale Carson[2] has easy-to-follow directions for appetizers, soups, chowders and stews, bread, fish and shellfish, fowl and game, vegetables, starches and side dishes, condiments and preserves, desserts, and beverages. Ms. Carson bases her recipes on traditional Native American foods such as corn, tomatoes, beans, squash, berries, maple syrup, varieties of game, meats and fowl, fish and shellfish, plus other foods that Native Americans worked into their own repertoire, such as apples, wheat and oat flour, leavening, dairy products, and eggs.

The author doesn't consider her book to be an authentic history of Native American food, because she does include elements that purists with expertise about Indigenous foods would omit. Instead she regards her book as a bridge to introduce Native American food traditions to the mainstream population.

She provides clear directions for preparing such dishes as oysters on the half shell, stuffed quahogs, mussels with lemon-butter (definitely not a Native American dish—this is bridge food), smoked halibut cheeks, and wild mushroom appetizer (she warns readers not to go picking wild mushrooms), to name only a few items. She herself loves to cook big, chewy portobello mushrooms to serve with buffalo, beef, veal, or oysters.

Dale Carson also invented a Native American–influenced antipasto that includes raw clams and oysters, smoked trout, grilled roasted herring, lobster and crab in cider-hazelnut vinaigrette, sliced buffalo sausage, and a few other items, such as pemmican, for which there are recipes in her book. You can use as few or as many of the above ingredients as you prefer. The antipasto can pass muster simply with marinated Jerusalem artichokes, tomatoes, roasted bell peppers, sautéed wild mushrooms, batter dipped greens, roasted corn on the cob (with the cobs cut in quarters), and walnut or hazelnut oil, chopped nuts, and minced herbs. (The book has recipes for all these ingredients.) Assemble the items on a large platter, drizzle with nut oil, sprinkle with chopped nuts and minced herbs, and serve. It will certainly make an impressive first course and add a special flair to your engagement or wedding celebration.

Among the soups included are Black Bean Soup with Native Herbs, Wild Rice Soup, Winter Root and Onion Soup, Sorrel Soup á la Sioux, Sweet Potato Soup with Corn and Chilies, Butternut Squash Soup, Watercress and Potato Soup, Buffalo Ragout, which can also be done with rump or eye of round beef, and Buffalo Sausage Stew with Roasted Barley and Onions.

There are Crawfish and Black Bean Cakes among the fish recipes. The game dishes include Roast Wild Duck with Blackberry Sauce, Smoked Wild Turkey, and recipes for venison and buffalo sausages, as well as many more.

There's a good recipe for succotash (corn and beans together). In the days of the Plymouth Colony in Massachusetts, succotash was a soup containing fowl as well as corn and beans. The author, who is of Abenaki tribal heritage, has a Cherokee friend who makes succotash with green beans, fresh tomatoes, onions, and corn kernels tossed with fresh herbs. The author grew up in the east, eating succotash with corn kernels, lima beans, butter, and cream.

The mushroom and salmon recipe that follows would be a very tasty appetizer at a wedding reception. This dish hints at authentic Native American food, while suggesting an elegance that could enhance anyone's dinner gathering.

MUSHROOMS STUFFED WITH
MISHQUAMMAUQUOCK (SALMON)

20 large fresh button mushrooms

1 teaspoon olive oil

2 chopped green onions or scallions

1 tablespoon finely chopped walnuts

1/2 teaspoon fresh dill weed

1/2 teaspoon soy sauce

1/4 teaspoon salt

Dash hot pepper sauce

2 ounces smoked or steamed salmon, flaked OR canned boneless, skinless pink salmon, drained, picked clean

Flat-leaf parsley, fresh minced for garnish

Clean the mushrooms and remove the stems and any dark spots.

Place the mushrooms, stem side up, around the edge of a glass pie plate. Cover with waxed paper and microwave for 3–4 minutes or until the mushrooms are almost tender and starting to render liquid. Alternatively, place the mushrooms in a baking container, cover, and bake at 350°F for 10 minutes. Invert the cooked mushrooms on paper towels to drain.

Combine the olive oil, onion, nuts, dill, soy sauce, salt, and hot pepper sauce in a bowl. Stir in the salmon.

Fill the mushroom caps with the salmon mixture, rounding the tops.

Place the filled mushrooms around the edge of the glass plate and microwave, uncovered, about 2 1/2 minutes, giving the plate a half turn midway through the cooking time. Alternatively, return the filled mushrooms to a 350°F oven and bake for 3–5 minutes or until the salmon mixture is bubbly.

Garnish with parsley. Serve immediately.

Makes 3–4 servings.

MAPLE-MUSTARD VINAIGRETTE

This distinctive salad dressing could also
enhance a first course of fresh greens.

1/3 cup olive oil
1/2 cup walnut oil
1/2 cup cider vinegar
2 tablespoons maple syrup
1 tablespoon coarse brown mustard
Salt and pepper

Combine all the ingredients in a small bowl and whisk until smooth and emulsified.

Pour into a small glass jar with a tight-fitting lid and store in the refrigerator for up to two weeks.

—::—

Powwows have spread the word about Apache fry bread. It can be served in its natural state or topped with honey or jam. Fry bread can be cooked with yeast, baking soda, oil, or butter.

FRY BREAD

Fry bread can definitely provide a surprising alternative to plain dinner rolls or Italian bread at any dinner gathering.

1 tablespoon vegetable oil, for frying
2¹/₂ cups flour (¹/₂ whole wheat, if possible)
1 teaspoon baking powder
¹/₂ teaspoon salt
1 teaspoon sugar
1 cup milk
1 teaspoon canola oil

Heat the oil in a skillet over medium-high heat until hot but not smoking. Combine the flour, baking powder, salt, and sugar in a large bowl. Stir in the milk and oil to make a dough. Shape into 8–10 disks about 5 inches in diameter. Fry the shaped dough in the hot oil until brown and crisp. Serve hot.

Makes 8–10 pieces.

—::—

Adding a taste of authentic Native American cuisine to a wedding dinner

Recipes for canapés and all sorts of appetizers, main courses, and side dishes, especially those made with corn, will add the natural, simple goodness of Indian cooking to your celebration. Visit your local bookstore or library to search for Native American cookbooks to get some more ideas for recipes.

It may be helpful to include menu cards on each table, describing the different dishes that will be served and their significance. Decorate the menu cards with traditional Native American drawings or patterns.

Instead of the traditional floral centerpiece on each table, why not create your own Native American-inspired centerpiece? You could include pumpkins, squashes, gourds, dried corn (perhaps different colors), dried peppers, and items from nature such as feathers, shells, beads, and leaves in handmade baskets. You may want to spread each table with a traditional cloth or handwoven tapestry and include traditional pottery, instruments, or other handicrafts as the centerpiece.

As a guest favor, you could make a little "book" including the recipes for the dishes that are served at the wedding reception. If you know the name of the recipe in the original language, you could add it for a special touch. You could include some traditional love poetry or love songs. Reproducing the work of Native American artists on the cover and binding the booklet with rattan will give your guests a unique souvenir of your celebration.

NOTES

1. *Native American Autobiography: An Anthology,* edited by Arnold Krupat (Madison: University of Wisconsin Press, 1994).

2. Dale Carson, *New Native American Cooking* (New York: Random House, 1996).

FASHIONS, JEWELRY, BASKETRY, CLOTH WEAVING, DECORATIONS

What do Native American women wear for their weddings?" a writer recently asked Georgetta Ryan, a reference librarian at the National Museum of the American Indian in New York.

"They wear their best stuff," she replied. She chose a magnificent silver and turquoise belt depicted in a book on the subject of fine Indian jewelry. "Men would wear that, too," she said. But Native American artists offer a vast number of praiseworthy choices. Everything depends on individual taste.

Native Americans have earned well-deserved international fame for basket making; weaving of cotton cloth and wool for clothes, blankets, and other decorative and utilitarian uses; preparation of animal skins for clothes and tents; and for their artistry as designers and jewelry makers. In the Southwest, the men were the cloth weavers, and they created designs—illustrations, really—of representative figures of people and animals. Women made the baskets, and their designs were usually abstract and geometrical.

—::—

All Native American tribes created and wore jewelry. Pieces could be made from beads, feathers, shells, fresh water pearls, carved wood, or other materials. The most distinctive of all was jewelry made from silver, turquoise, and coral. In the Southwest, the Zuni wrought magnificent, museum-quality jewelry. Their rings, necklaces, bracelets, belts, and other pieces can sell for very high prices. The Navajo may have become silversmiths before the Zuni in the nineteenth century, but the Zuni people developed their craft of jewelry making to such a high art that they influenced the techniques and imaginations of the top-notch Navajo jewelry makers.

The artistry of Native American jewelry makers has become a subject of serious study on the university level. The same is true of basketry, weaving, and visual design. Contemporary Native Americans have put their imprint on such items as bow ties and cummerbunds for bright, distinctive, formal evening wear. Often Indian arts and crafts are sold at powwows, as well as in stores and museum shops. A shop at the National Museum of the American Indian has a wide variety of items for home decoration and fashion wear, including the cummerbunds and bow ties.

In the Southwest, Indigenous women first wove baskets and worked in ceramics, making a wide variety of pots, jars, platters, and utensils. They actually began to develop their skills thousands of years ago, as did Native American women living far to the east.

By the time the first white settlers arrived in Indian lands, basketry, created by coiling, braiding, and twining, had become a highly developed art. Women also made mats, boxes, and bags to carry all kinds of tools. Women learned how to weave and seal baskets so tightly that they could hold water; when the women put hot rocks inside, these watertight baskets could cook food. Women were very inventive in making designs for baskets, some of which included beads and shells. All sorts of natural dyes were used to color their designs.

Indigenous people around the country also learned weaving and spinning with handlooms, probably from Europeans and particularly from Spaniards in the Southwest. Women often did the weaving work, too, except among the Hopi, as the Hopi men were the great weavers. They produced wool clothes and blankets, employing diverse materials, such as bird feathers and animal skins, to beautify their designs. Some weavers even used buffalo hair. In the Southwest, the Hopi wove cotton cloth, while other tribes wove different materials. Hopi brides wore cotton wedding dresses.

Native Americans became great artisans in the preparation of animal skins for clothes, moccasins, baskets, bags, tools, and tipis. Women wore the hides of buffalo, deer, antelope, and elk. Though Indians didn't use tannic acid, they had ingenious methods for tanning skins with animal and vegetable products. Their techniques required hard labor, and the results were of very high quality. White settlers marveled at the durability, softness, and light weight of the clothes and tipis. Men usually made the beads, but women worked them into designs for clothes and ornaments. When porcupine quills were available women often used them in embroidery designs on bags, pouches, clothes, and moccasins. Some pieces were made to order—that is, the men told the women which designs to custom tailor to the men's individual tastes.

Traditional Native American women enjoyed fashionable accessories. They adored beads, shells, feathers, and many types of decorations—the more exotic the better—to enhance their clothing and hair ornaments. "They were style conscious," summed up John Upton Terrell and Donna M. Terrell.[1]

"From the far north came beads of walrus ivory. From the eastern coast came beads made from clam, oyster, quahog, and periwinkle shells. From the subtropical south came beads made of wood, as well as of many kinds of oddly-shaped and highly colored shells. From the Southeast and the Midwest came fresh water pearls. From the Pacific Coast came exquisite beads of dentalium, abalone, and olivella shells. From the Rocky Mountains and the northern Great Plains came beads of animal teeth, among them the highly-valued milk teeth of the elk. From several regions came the claws of bears for pendants, and these were eagerly sought by tribes of the southern Great Plains and the Southwest. From the pueblos came the famous beads of turquoise, which so delighted all women," wrote the Terrells.

Native Americans also adorned their skins with tattoos and body paints. They turned animal fats and vegetable oils into hair and body oils, and grass and seeds into perfumes. Women loved bird trophies and feathers from regions far from their homes—for example, ivory billed woodpecker scalps, parakeet skins, wild turkey feathers, and feathers from tropical birds native to Mexico. "Feathers were good business anywhere," write the Terrells.

The Terrells also tell a story of the small Havasupai tribe, which was finally driven into an area of the Southwest by stronger, more numerous tribes. There they discovered a red ocher, which they began trading for other items they needed. Soon they became rich and famous for their high-priced red ocher used for cosmetics and ceremonial regalia.

Women used everything from bark and grass to animal skins for their clothing. Contrary to legend and lore, women dressed themselves with distinctive differences in designs among the tribes. A few tribes fancied hats woven of materials used for basketry.

They had divergent tastes in hairstyles, and women of different ages coifed their hair in styles appropriate for their age groups. Some women wore their hair in two masses or braids that fell in front of their shoulders. Others let their hair hang free down their backs and cut bangs across their foreheads. One observer in the Great Plains noticed that young Sioux girls wore braids down their back and tied them with pendants, while post-pubescent girls wore their hair above their shoulders. Some women wore decorated headbands. Some wore one braid down their backs. For the puberty ceremony, Hopi girls pulled their hair up into large whorls on each side of their heads. They may have been trying to imitate the shape of the squash blossom, that popular symbol of fertility. Some women never cut their hair at all and let it grow down past their knees.

Women found ways to tweeze their eyebrows with wooden implements or clam shells, and they painted their faces in symbolic, traditional, and individualist designs. In some tribes, women had large portions of their bodies tattooed; in others tattoos were kept to a minimum. Some designs seemed to mimic the patterns painted on pottery and woven into baskets. Men usually did the tattoo work, using everything from sharp flint instruments to cactus spines as needles, dabbling in black and red colors in particular, and sometimes blue. Most Native Americans in the modern world abandoned their customs and techniques for adorning their hair and bodies long ago.

Books on Indian Jewelry

Some of the books in the following list may be available in libraries and museums, particularly the Indian museums under the aegis of the Smithsonian Institution. Others may need to be ordered directly from publishers. These are only a sampling of the many books on the subject of Indian jewelry.

Bassman, Theda, and Michael Bassman. *Zuni Jewelry*. West Chester, PA: Schiffer Publishing Ltd., 1992. This book has exquisite illustrations of jewelry, such as a squash blossom necklace with matching earrings and a ring made of mother-of-pearl, tortoise shell, and coral. The publisher notes that a free catalogue is available. The book can be purchased directly from them (Schiffer Publishing Ltd., 4880 Lower Valley Road, Atgien, PA 19310) and at bookstores.

Branson, Oscar T. *Indian Jewelry Making*, Volumes I and II. Tucson, AZ: Treasure Chest Publications, Inc., Vol. I, 1977, and Vol. II, 1979. These books depict fine examples of squash blossom jewelry, which has been wrought in countless variations of the basic theme. The books also have illustrations of Hopi and Santa Clara Pueblo wedding jugs, and other miniature silver pottery. You can contact the publisher directly at Treasure Chest Publications, Inc., PO Box 5250, Tucson, AZ 85703.

Indian Arts and Crafts Association and the Council for Indigenous Arts and Culture. *Collecting Authentic Indian Arts and Crafts*. Summertown, TN: Native Voices, Book Publishing Company, 1999. A unique team of American Indian artists and experts explain techniques used to produce and identify authentic Native American silver jewelry, beadwork, quillwork, pottery, rugs, baskets, fetishes, and katsina dolls. Individual copies are available from Mail Order Catalog, PO Box 180, Summertown, TN 38483, (800) 695-2241.

Schiffer, Peter N. *Indian Jewelry on the Market*. San Francisco: Schiffer Publishing Ltd., 1996. Though not specifically about jewelry, this history book contains a fine photo of a Zuni squash blossom necklace, which was made by a father for his daughter at the time of her marriage. He told her that her children would surround her, and the necklace was the symbol of her fertility.

—::—

Including Indian jewelry and crafts in a contemporary wedding

Native American jewelry is usually for sale in stores in major American cities, particularly stores specializing in Indian arts and crafts, and, of course, at powwows. See the information resources section, page 119, for places that can refer you to stores, jewelry makers, and other outlets for authentic Native American jewelry.

Perhaps the bride and groom would want to wear some pieces of traditional jewelry. There are Native American artists and jewelry makers who could create wedding bands with traditional patterns and designs on them.

Even if the bride opts for a Western-style white wedding dress, she could easily wear Native American jewelry with it. Turquoise jewelry, in particular, would be striking against a white dress—not to mention the fact that it fulfills the requirement for wearing "something blue."

A bride and groom may choose to give their wedding attendants (bridesmaids, flower girls, groomsmen, and ushers) a piece of Native American jewelry as a gift. Bridesmaids would certainly enjoy bracelets or earrings, while groomsmen may enjoy handcrafted belt buckles or silver and turquoise cuff links, tie tacks, or money clips. Such gifts would also be perfect for parents and grandparents.

NOTE

1. John Upton Terrell and Donna M. Terrell, *Indian Women of the Western Morning: Their Life in Early America* (New York: Anchor Books, 1976).

POSTSCRIPT: DIVORCE AND REMARRIAGE

*F*ools Crow, the Teton Sioux man from South Dakota who became engaged and married to his wife, Fannie, in a short period of time—perhaps as little as one night—simply by collecting her possessions and taking them to his own camp, became a widower in 1954 after thirty-eight years in a happy marriage. For four years, he lived alone as a bachelor. But one day the daughter of a friend of his came to him and said her mother, Kate, a widow, was lonely. Her family thought it would be a very good idea if Fools Crow married her. Wasn't he ever lonely? Kate's daughter wanted to know. Yes, he was, he said.

He decided to marry Kate, and with her he lived very happily, too. She had never been off the reservation; he began to take her traveling, and she enjoyed the adventure. Fools Crow's marriages were blessedly unmarred by any kind of strife. In recounting the tale of his second marriage to Thomas E. Mails for the book *Fools Crow*, he leaves out any mention of a wedding feast or a bride-price. These rites rarely came up for second marriages unless the brides were still quite young. In Kate's case, she was already well into middle age, and so was Fools Crow.

Not all Native Americans enjoyed such serene domestic lives. Divorce was commonly practiced among Indigenous peoples.

Some, such as the Oglala Sioux, had rather complicated procedures for divorce, but most divorces were simple affairs, or they could be. A woman put her husband's possessions outside the house. Or the woman went home to her own family. Or the man simply left home one day and never returned.

In some tribes, women remarried many times, either because they were divorced or widowed. Each time they remarried, of course, they didn't have to go through all the elaborate gift giving and mighty preparations as they had done for their first marriages. The older a woman was, the less complicated the customs and traditions were. Everyone just wanted to be happy.

For further reading about the family customs, structures, and traditions of Native Americans, see the bibliography, pages 120–21.

INFORMATION RESOURCES

1. American Indian Community House, 708 Broadway, New York, NY 10003. Phone: (212) 598-0100.

2. National Museum of the American Indian, The George Gustav Heye Center, One Bowling Green, New York, NY 10004. Phone: (212) 514-3700. This museum is under the auspices of the Smithsonian Institution.

3. National Museum of the American Indian, The Cultural Resources Center, 4220 Silver Road, Suitland, MD 20746. Phone: (301) 238-6624 Fax: (301) 238-3200. This center is also under the auspices of the Smithsonian Institution.

4. National Museum of the American Indian on the National Mall Museum, Washington, DC 20560. Phone: (202) 633-1000, www.nmai.si.edu.

5. Louis Mofsie, founder and leader of the Thunderbird American Indian Dancers, teaches dance and beadwork at the American Indian Community House, 708 Broadway, New York, NY 10003. Call the American Indian Community House, (212) 598-0100, or the National Museum of the American Indian, (212) 514-3700, for information about scheduled performances and classes.

—::—

Photo facing page:
Maza Win (Mah-zah-we) poses with her new spouse, Opawinge "One Hundred" on their wedding day. Picture taken at the Post Office building in Stephan, South Dakota, by Father Ambrose Mattingly. Courtesy American Indian Culture Research Center, Marvin, South Dakota.

BIBLIOGRAPHY

Bailey, Flora L. *Some Sex Beliefs and Practices in a Navaho Community*. Cambridge, MA: Peabody Museum of American Archaeology and Ethnology, Harvard University, 1950. This rare book is available in some Harvard University libraries and at the National Museum of the American Indian in New York.

Dancing Colors: Paths of Native American Women. Compiled by C. J. Brafford and Laine Thom. San Francisco: Chronicle Books, 1992.

Driver, Harold E. *Indians of North America*. Revised 2nd edition. Chicago: University of Chicago Press, 1969.

Encyclopedia of North American Indians. Edited by Frederick E. Hoxie. Boston: Houghton Mifflin Company, 1996.

An Ethnology Dictionary of the Navajo Language. Saint Michaels, AZ: The Franciscan Fathers, 1910.

Ewers, John C. *The Blackfeet: Raiders of the Northwestern Plains*. Norman: University of Oklahoma Press, 1958.

Handbook of the North American Indian. General editor, William C. Sturtevant. Washington, DC: Smithsonian Institution, 1978. A twenty-volume encyclopedia summarizing knowledge about Native peoples north of Mesoamerica, including linguistics. Each of the volumes includes one or more chapters on the languages of that area.

Hill, Sarah H. *Weaving New Worlds: Southeastern Cherokee Women and Their Basketry*, Chapel Hill: University of North Carolina Press, 1997.

The Indian Peoples of Eastern America: A Documentary History of the Sexes. Edited by James Axtell. New York: Oxford University Press, 1981.

Iroquois Women: An Anthology. Edited by William Guy Spittal. Ontario: Iroqrafts, Ltd., Iroquois Publications, 1996.

Mails, Thomas E. *Fools Crow*. Lincoln: University of Nebraska Press, 1979.

Mankiller, Wilma and Michael Wallis. *Mankiller: A Chief and Her People*. Revised. New York: St. Martin's Press, 1999.

Mooney, James. *Myths of the Cherokee and Sacred Formulas of the Cherokees* (reprint, Nashville, TN: Charles and Randy Elder, 1982).

Native American Autobiography: An Anthology. Edited by Arnold Krupat. Madison: University of Wisconsin Press, 1994.

Niethammer, Carolyn. *Daughters of the Earth: The Lives and Legends of American Indian Women*. New York: Touchstone, 1977.

Page, Susanne and Jake Page. *Hopi*. New York: Abradale Press and Harry N. Abrams, Inc., 1992.

—— *Navajo*. New York: Harry N. Abrams Publishers, 1995.

Rasmussen, William M. S., and Robert S. Tilton. *Pocahontas: Her Life and Legend*. Richmond: Virginia Historical Society, 1994.

Stockel, H. Henrietta. *Women of the Apache Nation*. Reno: University of Nevada Press, 1991.

Terrell, John Upton and Donna M. Terrell. *Indian Women of the Western Morning*. New York: Anchor Books, 1976.

Trigger, Bruce G., and Wilcomb E. Washburn. *Cambridge History of the Native Peoples of the Americas*. Vols. 1 and 2. New York: Cambridge University Press, 1996.

Walker, James R. *Lakota Society*. Lincoln: University of Nebraska Press, 1982.

Witherspoon, Gary. *Navajo Kinship and Marriage*. Chicago: University of Chicago Press, 1975.

The Woman's Way. Edited by Time-Life. Alexandria, VA: Time-Life Books, 1995.

Index

Native Voices

tribal legends, medicine, arts & crafts,
history, life experiences, spirituality

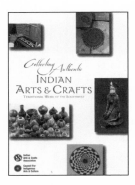

**Collecting Authentic
Indian Arts & Crafts**
IACA and CIAC
1-57067-062-5
$16.95

Sisters in Spirit
Iroquois Influence on
Early American Feminists
Sally Roesch Wagner
1-57067-121-4 $14.95

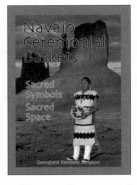

**Navajo Ceremonial
Baskets**
Georgianna Simpson
1-57067-118-4
$19.95

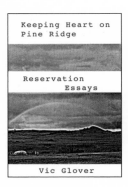

**Keeping Heart
on Pine Ridge**
Vic Glover
1-57067-165-6 $16.95

**The World of Chief
Seattle**
How Can One Sell the Air?
Warren Jefferson
1-57067-095-1 $13.95

**Basic Call to
Consciousness**
Revised edition
1-57067-159-1 $11.95

Purchase these Native American titles from your local bookstore
or you can buy them directly from:

Book Publishing Company • P.O. Box 99 • Summertown, TN 38483
1-800-695-2241

Please include $3.95 per book for shipping and handling.